DELIVE
BENEFI

BCS, THE CHARTERED INSTITUTE FOR IT

BCS, The Chartered Institute for IT, is committed to making IT good for society. We use the power of our network to bring about positive, tangible change. We champion the global IT profession and the interests of individuals engaged in that profession, for the benefit of all.

Exchanging IT expertise and knowledge

The Institute fosters links between experts from industry, academia and business to promote new thinking, education and knowledge sharing.

Supporting practitioners

Through continuing professional development and a series of respected IT qualifications, the Institute seeks to promote professional practice tuned to the demands of business. It provides practical support and information services to its members and volunteer communities around the world.

Setting standards and frameworks

The Institute collaborates with government, industry and relevant bodies to establish good working practices, codes of conduct, skills frameworks and common standards. It also offers a range of consultancy services to employers to help them adopt best practice.

Become a member

Over 70,000 people including students, teachers, professionals and practitioners enjoy the benefits of BCS membership. These include access to an international community, invitations to a roster of local and national events, career development tools and a quarterly thought-leadership magazine. Visit www.bcs.org/membership to find out more.

Further Information
BCS, The Chartered Institute for IT,
First Floor, Block D,
North Star House, North Star Avenue,
Swindon, SN2 1FA, United Kingdom.
T +44 (0) 1793 417 424
F +44 (0) 1793 417 444
www.bcs.org/contact

http://shop.bcs.org/

DELIVERING BENEFIT
Technical leadership capabilities

Brian Sutton and Robina Chatham

Published by BCS Learning & Development Ltd, a wholly owned subsidiary of BCS, The Chartered Institute for IT, First Floor, Block D, North Star House, North Star Avenue, Swindon, SN2 1FA, UK. www.bcs.org

ISBN: 978-1-78017-39-86
PDF ISBN: 978-1-78017-38-32
ePUB ISBN: 978-1-78017-38-49
Kindle ISBN: 978-1-78017-38-56

Ebook available

British Cataloguing in Publication Data.
A CIP catalogue record for this book is available at the British Library.

Disclaimer:
The views expressed in this book are of the author(s) and do not necessarily reflect the views of the Institute or BCS Learning & Development Ltd except where explicitly stated as such. Although every care has been taken by the author(s) and BCS Learning & Development Ltd in the preparation of the publication, no warranty is given by the author(s) or BCS Learning & Development Ltd as publisher as to the accuracy or completeness of the information contained within it and neither the author(s) nor BCS Learning & Development Ltd shall be responsible or liable for any loss or damage whatsoever arising by virtue of such information or any instructions or advice contained within this publication or by any of the aforementioned.

BCS books are available at special quantity discounts to use as premiums and sale promotions, or for use in corporate training programmes. Please visit our 'Contact us' page at www.bcs.org/contact

Publisher's acknowledgements
Reviewer: John Anfield
Publisher: Ian Borthwick
Commissioning Editor: Rebecca Youé
Production Manager: Florence Leroy
Project Manager: Sunrise Setting Ltd
Cover work: Alexander Wright
Picture credits: Shutterstock © sezer66

Typeset by Lapiz Digital Services, Chennai, India.
Printed and bound by Henry Ling Limited, at the Dorset Press, Dorchester, DT1 1HD

CONTENTS

LIST OF FIGURES

ABOUT THE AUTHORS

Professor Brian Sutton has over 40 years' management and leadership experience. He has developed comprehensive information systems (IS) strategies, conducted large-scale re-engineering initiatives and led major organisational change. He regularly contributes articles to professional journals and speaks at major professional gatherings. He holds a Doctorate in Corporate Education, a Master's degree in Information Systems Management from the London School of Economics and has worked extensively in both the private and public sectors in Europe and the United States. He was formerly a Professor of Systems Management in the Information Resources Management College of the National Defence University in Washington, DC. He is currently Professor of Learning Performance in the Faculty of Professional and Social Sciences at Middlesex University.

Dr Robina Chatham has over 35 years' experience in IT. She has held positions that range from IT project manager within the shipbuilding industry to European Chief Information Officer for a leading merchant bank and lecturer at Cranfield School of Management. She is qualified as both a Mechanical Engineer and a Neuroscientist. Previous books include *Corporate Politics for IT Managers: How to Get Streetwise*; *Changing the IT Leader's Mindset: Time for Revolution rather than Evolution*; and *The Art of IT Management: Practical Tools and Techniques*. Robina now runs her own company specialising in management development and executive coaching. She is also a visiting fellow at Cranfield School of Management and a research associate for the Leading Edge Forum. Her prime focus is on helping senior IT managers to increase their personal impact and influence at board level.

FOREWORD

I am going to start my introduction to this new book by Robina and Brian by quoting Stephen Covey in his book *The 7 Habits of Highly Effective People* (2004): 'Start with the end in mind', a fairly innocuous but hugely powerful statement once you learn how to truly exploit the meaning of it. We will come back to this later.

I first met Robina early in my career at a point where I had chosen to take redundancy from an IT leadership role I loved, in an organisation that was preparing itself for sale. At that time, I had a choice: to stay and work for the outsourced partner I had selected or to take redundancy. Both paths were unknown to me; each held possibilities but no certainties, and from that moment forwards the one constant in my career, like many others in the IT industry, has been the ability to 'navigate the grey' and derive possibilities from planned and unplanned events and opportunities.

While transitioning to my new role I chose to attend a course at Cranfield School of Management, called 'Organisational Politics and IT', the basis of which would evolve into what we now know as business engagement or business relationship management (it was, however, many years before the IT profession even had a formal name for it).

The course was led by Dr Robina Chatham and the beauty (and discomfort) of the content was that it took me away from all of the functional skills I had grown up with and been rewarded for in this industry. These were the skills that were highly valued by my then mentors and functional senior leaders: analysis, coding, scripting and devising strategy documents that were like the Encyclopaedia Britannica and would soon become dust-gathering shelfware. From this background and through attending this course I transitioned to a world of personality types, colleague engagement, challenger relationships, building trust, developing business understanding and alignment and developing novel capabilities within IT teams, including myself. Although I didn't know it at the time, this learning uniquely positioned me to transform a variety of businesses, as well as shaping the career path for myself and many others since.

Back to 'start with the end in mind'. Robina and Brian in this book reflect on this fundamental principle by posing the question, what does good look like for you, your team, your organisation and your industry? Using their personal experience, expertise and insight, they have created a very practical and useable guide to improving your working environment, increasing the value of your contribution and enhancing the quality of the legacy you leave behind.

This book will support you in creating the right environment, relationships, strategies, thinking, communication material and most importantly the team that will allow you to define your own version of 'start with the end in mind'. It doesn't just talk about the theories that can be used; it takes you by the hand and asks you to join Robina and Brian on the journey, but, as with all good things in life, to do it justice you and your teams may have to 'dig deep'. Throughout the journey, Robina and Brian are there to help you ask the right question, then the next, and the next and the one after that of yourself, your team and your colleagues.

What makes Robina and Brian's book so powerful is that they tell you 'how' to create your version of 'start with the end in mind', using their many years of real life experience and the invaluable insights provided by senior IT leaders they have worked with over the years. You may even recognise some of them.

I would always encourage you to create your own vision, but use this book as a touchstone along the way – go be everything you can be. This IT industry of ours has some great leaders but always needs more 'kick ass' business leaders who are digitally aware and agile, who are able to navigate the grey, who can build great teams and leave great legacies.

In a future where our opportunities to contribute become limitless and the demands on our businesses increase, we are here to serve, to transform, but most importantly, to contribute as business leaders who just happen to have a digital specialism. Enjoy!

Tanya Foster-Fitzgerald FBCS
Chief Information Officer, Raytheon

ACKNOWLEDGEMENTS

We would like to offer our sincere thanks to all the people who have attended our training courses around the world. You have inspired and motivated us to produce this work; the shape and content of this book came about as a direct result of your questions. So, when we sat down to write this book, we did not ask ourselves 'What do we know that we wish to tell other people?' Instead, we have built this book around your questions and the answers that you inspired in us, as we struggled to find the best ways of guiding you in your unique challenges. Without you, this book would never have seen the light of day.

To those of you who are familiar with our work, we hope that you will find renewed value in hearing again the ideas that we tried so hard to convey as we answered your questions. To those who are coming to us for the first time, we hope that some of the content will inspire you to see and be different and to find new understanding in your working relationships.

Last, but by no means least, we need to say a huge thank you to our respective partners, Angela and John. They are a constant support, and without their patience and understanding we could never have completed this book.

PREFACE

Most people who find themselves in a leadership position for the first time are lost and unprepared. The challenge of stepping up to leadership is not something that can be overcome by attending a course or reading a book that abstractly talks about planning or motivation or delegation. There is a big difference between understanding the theory of how something works and being able to apply those ideas in practice, especially if things are going wrong and you are under pressure to get results.

We work extensively with mid- and senior-level leaders in the IT sector across national boundaries and cultures. We find common issues whether we are working with technical team leaders or the senior leadership team; they all ask us similar questions and they always start with the words 'How do I ...?'

But we have come to realise that generally they are not asking for theory; they already have the knowledge of what to do, they just have no idea of how to go about doing it in their particular context.

When you engage with someone as their leader, you are not simply directing work; you are engaged in creating and sustaining an environment within which those people can deploy their various talents to collectively achieve great outcomes – outcomes that make a real difference in the lives of business partners, clients, customers and constituents.

Successful leaders realise that success comes more through their ability to create and sustain positive emotional spaces for their people than from implementing best-practice processes.

Every situation that you face as a leader will have an element of uniqueness; every interaction will be coloured by the hopes, fears and aspirations of all parties. What makes leadership so difficult is that all too often you are unaware of your own driving forces, let alone those that drive the people you are leading.

When we are consulting with IT leaders at all levels we hear the same complaints: too much work, too few resources, too much change, conflicting priorities and customers who don't understand our problems. We see good people running faster just to stay in the same place and too many people facing burnout. It need not be like this, but it takes courage and focus from the leader to change the situation for everyone's benefit. In this book, we look at six areas of focus that we have come to believe are critical to an IT leader's ability to deliver business benefit. The first thing to realise is that no leader can make a difference alone. To make a difference you need your team to follow your lead, to willingly commit their time, effort and talents to achieve great outcomes for your customers and business partners.

We use the term business partner purposefully; historically IT functions have primarily served the back office and adopted the role of 'service provider'; however, the world has changed. IT now pervades all areas of our organisations – front and back office – it is seen as the prime means of improving front-of-the-firm effectiveness and, in many cases, the catalyst for business transformation. As a consequence, IT's mindset is shifting from service provider to 'business partner'. In this new world, traditional IT measures are no longer appropriate – they are akin to asking for a prenup in that they can be a major sign of distrust. Research conducted in 2016 by the Leading Edge Forum found traditional IT measures to be holding many organisations back; the value placed on control and proof rooting them firmly in provider mode. The more enlightened organisations had let go of these traditional measures and, in an environment of mutual trust and understanding, relied on qualitative as opposed to quantitative measures.

Indeed, those organisations operating in partner mode viewed formal measurements as not only irrelevant but also offensive. This research indicates that as the IT function moves centre stage towards trusted business partners, the approach to demonstrating business benefit must also move to adopt these more qualitative measures. In this book, we take the stance that the best way to envisage business benefit is by adopting the mindset of the business partner. All six chapters in this book set out from this perspective.

Key to delivering benefit is really getting to know how technology can help your business better serve its customers. Therefore in Chapter 1 we start with understanding your customer and how to delight them. Getting close to your customers and ensuring you are 'easy to do business with' are key factors, but this requires you to look beyond just the immediate horizon of what is consuming their energies in the moment. As such, Chapter 2 deals with developing your ability to see the bigger picture. With a clear idea of how what you are doing fits with the overall long-term strategy of your organisation you are better placed to engineer solutions that have lasting impact. When you understand where you are going and you work with your head up rather than your eyes down it becomes possible to see developing trends or take advantage of unexpected events. For this reason, in Chapter 3 we look at how you can get better at seeing new opportunities. The ability to really exploit new opportunities will almost certainly call for you and your team to develop novel approaches; therefore in Chapter 4 we look at ways in which you can build a spirit of innovation within your team.

If you are successful in developing the skills and attitudes that we have identified in the first four chapters, the net result will be lots of new opportunities to bring about changes in your business that are focused on improving the experience for all of your customers and other stakeholders. As a leader, it is important that you are seen as someone who can make change happen; this is the focus of Chapter 5. In the final chapter, we turn our attention to what you can personally do to help everyone involved cope better with the personal and organisational impacts of deep and profound changes in their working lives.

Each of the chapters follows the same structure. Each chapter contains short anecdotes of how real people have applied some of the ideas in this book. We point to resources for you to develop a deeper engagement and understanding and we provide a series of simple things you can do now to start to develop into a more successful team leader.

Throughout the book you will see icons in the margin to focus your attention to particular aspects. Below you will find the key.

GOLDEN RULE

The golden rule to remember, even if you don't remember anything else about the chapter.

ANECDOTE

An anecdote or case study; real-life experience from leaders who have faced these situations and taken purposeful action.

KEY IDEA

Key ideas to unlock potential. Things you should be trying to build into your professional practice.

QUESTIONS TO ASK YOURSELF

Get into the habit of asking yourself these questions before you take action.

EXERCISE REGIMES

Things you can try immediately together with hints on how to adopt and adapt the ideas to your unique situation.

RESOURCES

Links to resources where you can find additional helpful and inspiring ideas.

We are always fascinated to hear of your experiences in applying the ideas we have presented. Please email us with examples from your personal experience and we will seek to include them in future editions of this book series.

Brian Sutton and Robina Chatham

drbriansutton@gmail.com
robina@chatham.uk.com

1 UNDERSTANDING YOUR CUSTOMERS: HOW TO TRULY DELIGHT THEM

The focus of this chapter is learning to look at the business through the eyes of your customers or clients. Often as you grapple with the challenges of your daily tasks and activities it is easy to lose sight of how those tasks contribute to the fulfilment of a customer or client need. Without customers a business cannot survive; therefore it is important to really understand how everything you do contributes to delivering a benefit that will be appreciated by a customer or client.

WHY IS THIS IMPORTANT?

Now you have stepped up to team leadership you will inevitably become more externally focused; your interactions with other business functions will increase and you should also start to interact externally with the customers or clients of your business. As an IT team leader, your prime reason for being is to help your business serve its customers or clients better or more effectively.

Any business will only survive if it is able to encourage existing customers to repeat purchase while at the same time finding new clients. Loyalty is the magic ingredient that drives repeat business and crucially encourages existing customers or clients to actively promote your goods or services and hence act as an unpaid sales force to help grow your business. If you are reading this and thinking that this doesn't apply to you as you provide an internal service to your peers in the rest of the business, remember unless you are seen as value for money and easy to do business with, you are always in danger of being outsourced.

All customers are important whether they are internal or external to the business and at some point a chain of internal customers or 'business partners' will have an interface with the outside world of real paying customers. In the early 1980s, Jan Carlzon became CEO of the problem-ridden Scandinavian Airlines. Over a period of 10 years he transformed the company by focusing on what he called 'Moments of Truth' – every interaction with a customer is an opportunity to form or change their impression of your business and your commitment to fulfilling their needs.

Your aim is to interact with your customers in a way that builds loyalty so that you become their supplier of choice (even if they don't have a choice).

In order to become the supplier of choice you will need to:

- Relentlessly focus on the customers' needs rather than your own.

- Understand that your customers also have customers. How is what you are doing going to help them with their own 'moments of truth'?

- Make sure that you are easy to do business with (ETDBW).[1]

In order to really excel you need to look along the value chain of the business, past your immediate business partner and try to understand how what you are providing will influence and enable your customers' customer to have a better experience.

---

[1] ETDBW is a term coined by Michael Hammer and expanded in his book *The Agenda: What Every Business Must Do to Dominate the Decade* (2001). It refers to being flexible as a business and not forcing your customers to do everything your way, using your processes and nomenclature. Being ETDBW means that you place the customers' needs first and are prepared to work differently to ensure they have a great experience.

THE IMPACT OF THE ISSUE

It is far more difficult to please customers of a service offering than those of a product offering. We expect services to work and when they do we don't give them a second thought; however, when they go wrong we are very quick to complain. Therefore, when delivering a service offering you will have to work twice as hard to delight your customers in comparison to someone with a product offering.

Many IT people are excited by the technology itself whereas their customers tend to be interested in what the technology can do for them. Salespeople used to focus on product features to distinguish the credentials of their offering, but now it is increasingly realised that customers are less interested in the features of a product than the solution that the product will allow them to achieve. As Harvard Professor Theodore Levitt reputedly used to tell his students, 'people don't want to buy a quarter inch drill, they want a quarter inch hole'. The typical IT professional is driven more by intellectual curiosity than a desire to serve. They get frustrated by business partners who don't know what they want, who can't make up their mind and change priorities, causing plans to be redrawn. They have a desire to pin requirements down to the nth degree as soon as possible, so they can get on to the real and interesting work: the intellectual challenge of getting the technology to do what they want it to do and pushing the boundaries of what is technically possible.

Consider a motor car for example; a feature of that car may be that it has a large engine; the advantage of that large engine is that it allows you to drive quickly, but this only translates into a benefit if you want to go quickly. Road safety, fuel economy or space for luggage and kids, for example, may be far more important to you than speed. The trick is to think in terms of benefit as opposed to features, i.e. the 'job to be done'.

3

In the world of IT, people are very good at thinking in terms of features, as these are tangible; however, the result is often technology for the sake of technology. Consider Microsoft's Office product for example – what percentage of its features do you use on a daily basis? For most people, it is probably less than 10 per cent. Only a small minority of people will be excited by the technology and its possibilities. The key is to maintain a clear focus on the purpose of the interaction with the customer: what is the customer trying to achieve and how can you make that as easy and as beneficial as possible?

MAKING SENSE OF IT ALL

Everyone understands that over the last 20 years the internet and then Web 2.0[2] has transformed the way that all organisations do business and changed attitudes forever by blurring the lines between what a business does for their customers and what the customers can do for themselves when interacting with that business.

We would like to draw your attention to three aspects that might, in the first instance, appear to be unrelated to understanding your customer, but we hope that you will see how they have created a new operating environment and are fundamental to building loyalty and trust in all customer interactions.

First, starting in the late 1990s, the internet brought about what Don Tapscott and Art Caston predicted in their landmark book *Paradigm Shift* (1993), namely **disintermediation, aka the removal of intermediaries**. In the 1990s the only way to book an airline ticket was through a travel agent; the way you taxed your car was to visit the Post Office with reams of documentary evidence. In this first wave of disintermediation, the intermediaries, who had traditionally acted as a buffer

---

[2] The term 'Web 2.0' was popularised by Tim O'Reilly and Dale Dougherty at the O'Reilly Media Web 2.0 Conference in late 2004. It refers to an end user experience that is characterised by user-generated content, usability and interoperability across platforms and devices.

between the consumer and the business provider largely providing an administrative service, found that their reason for being had disappeared overnight. Now it is common for both internal and external customers to be able to conduct all their standard business interactions using self-service methods. This has transformed both customer interactions and expectations; people now expect to do these things 24/7 when it suits them. This self-service interaction is often the first 'moment of truth' in a customer's experience and it needs to be seamless and simple.

Some companies have mastered the art of customer focus and as a result have become exceedingly successful, for example eBay with instant purchases, Uber with instant driver hire or Apple with booking customer appointments with Apple advisors. Other companies, however, still have work to do and often cause anguish and annoyance by taking their customers through many levels of a telephone menu without an appropriate option to choose from, or have websites with incomprehensible options, links that fail to work and security levels so complicated that a genuine customer struggles to complete their interaction.

Second, the **appearance of social media and** related applications allows us to instantly share images, ideas, news and opinions with large groups of people, many of whom you may not actually know, from anywhere at any time of the day. Each of the recipients of the messages can then discuss or share them with even more people. This ability has transformed the world of customer feedback. It used to be said that the British didn't like to complain; perhaps more accurately we should have said the British are reluctant to create a scene by complaining. Now that social media has removed the need for embarrassing physical confrontation we find that the British and every other nation under the sun are only too ready to share their major and minor sources of dissatisfaction with anyone and everyone. This, aligned to the psychological fact that people are far more likely to moan about perceived bad products or service than to praise good or even excellent ones, makes it more difficult than ever to build and maintain customer loyalty.

Some years ago, before the advent of social media, I visited a client organisation and as I entered one senior manager's office I noticed an A3 poster on the wall. It was quite professionally printed and had a large picture of a pencil, underneath which were the words 'IT support'. I later discovered that this same poster had pride of place on the walls of many of the organisation's senior leaders. As an outsider, I could see the funny side of this silent protest but if I had been the IT director I would have been looking for a new job. In a world dominated by instant communication, dissatisfaction of this level can destroy customer loyalty and make it pretty much impossible to create any semblance of a good working relationship.

Third, many traditional customer service interactions such as fault reporting and diagnostics are going DIY. Huge cost savings can be achieved by **removing face-to-face and telephone interaction**. In the article 'Kick Ass Customer Service', Dixon et al. (2017) suggest that it is possible to reduce the cost of an interaction from around £12 to just a few pence. Nowadays, many organisations routinely encourage their customers to fix their own problems by providing helpful web guides and, of course, YouTube videos.

New electric vehicles automatically download software updates and monitor their own performance, scheduling routine maintenance as needed without any intervention from the owner.

This level of do-it-yourself service is demonstrated in a proof of concept video produced by SAP,[3] that shows

---

[3] The video is available to licensed customers only unfortunately.

a woman discovering a broken switch on her washing machine. She uses an app on her smartphone to identify the product by QR code and then photographs the switch. An order is automatically placed for the replacement part, which is printed locally on a 3D printer; and she gets a text message to advise her the time the new part will be delivered to her door.

The result of this is that customers only interact directly with an organisation when they have exhausted all other channels; human-to-human interaction becomes the last resort and when it eventually takes place, the customer is already in a bad mood and looking for someone to vent their frustration on. Even if the customer's problem is solved, they may still resort to social media afterwards to tell the world how useless an organisation is.

Contrast the outstanding and simple customer service of the previous anecdote with that which we all too often experience. I (Robina) lost my smartphone once. I tried to phone the manufacturer to find out how to wipe the data and couldn't get through the first 'line of defence', which was to input the serial number of my phone which I didn't have because it was lost.

As a small business owner I am encouraged by the government to do everything online. I am told that there is lots of 'helpful' information online and that it is correct, but there is so much information that it is a lengthy and soul-destroying task to sort the wheat from the chaff. I find a lot of information telling me what I need to do, why I need to do it and the consequences if I don't, but what I lack is the basics, i.e. what button do I need to press in order to do what I need to do?

We have discussed three technological trends that have changed ideas about customer service forever, whether those customers are external to the business or internal business partners. Ironically, it is IT that has unleashed this monster, it is IT that continues to build ever more interactive services that exacerbate the situation and it is IT people who are probably the least well equipped to deal with human problems of their own making. To summarise, these three global technological trends have contributed to a situation where IT:

- routinely gives their customers direct access into back office systems;

- expects customers to perform many tasks for themselves, largely driven by a desire to reduce IT transaction costs;

- has made it difficult for its customers to interact directly with them unless and until they really have no other option;

- has enabled its customers to have at hand the means to share with the whole world how frustrated they are with IT's service;

- often gives its customers features they don't want or need in an attempt to delight them rather than focusing on the customers' 'job to be done'.

Thinking back to the idea that people are more willing to complain than praise leads to the rather counterintuitive idea that the primary route to customer loyalty is not through purely delighting our customers but also, more importantly, reducing their effort (the work they have to do to get their problem solved or their request for service fulfilled) (Dixon et al., 2010). This is tangentially related to the idea pioneered by Frederick Reichheld of Net Promoter (Reichheld, 2003), which, put simply, suggests that what counts in building loyalty is that you need more people spontaneously singing your praises than you have detractors; detractors are people who are actively advertising your inadequacies. Given the rise of social media and the fact that it is human nature to publicise bad news over good, getting to a point where you have more promoters than detractors can be challenging. In service centres, research shows that customers are four times more likely to leave a service interaction feeling disloyal than loyal (Dixon et al., 2010). We have no reason to believe that this statistic is fundamentally different in an internal context when considering routine IT–business partner interactions.

PRACTICAL ADVICE

The first step on the way to building and sustaining great customer relationships that create loyalty is to adopt an unrelenting focus on positive outcomes. Generally, customers are not really interested in the work you are doing to fulfil their needs; they don't care about your processes or your data management strategy; what they care about is their ability to serve their own customers, deliver benefit and achieve their desired outcomes. You need to make their desired outcome your fundamental driver. We suggest that your starting point is to adopt the following two strategies.

Work to become outcome focused

First make sure that in all your conversations with your team members you become the customers' champion. Place the needs of the customer above the needs of your own departmental processes or what may appear to the customer to be arcane methods and practices. As a result of disintermediation, layers have been removed and staff who in the past would have been insulated from external customers now find themselves in direct contact with them, or at least are building systems that may be accessed by external customers. These customers are not familiar with the internal processes or jargon and their expectations of service standards are set not by their interaction with them but by the experience of eBay, Uber and the like.

You need to get each and every one of your staff to view life through the eyes of their customers. A useful tool is to map the 'customer journey'; that is, every touch point where you engage with the customer before, during and after your contracted delivery. Start with your key customers or stakeholders; draw a map or diagram that shows every point of contact, every 'moment of truth'. You need to understand what takes place at each touch point, what you are asking of your customer and how difficult you are currently making that interaction; also, whether the interaction can be achieved in one touch or if you need multiple touches and multiple channels. What are the customers' overall impressions of how easy it is to do business with you at each touch point and what really frustrates them about the process? Your aim is to identify every opportunity you have to reduce the amount of effort and time the customer needs to expend to complete the interaction.

Second, you need to have a better understanding of what the customer is trying to achieve as a result of employing your products or services. What benefit and ultimate outcome are they seeking? A useful tool that has emerged largely through the shift to agile development methods is the 'user story'; this is an outcome-focused representation of the user's requirements. As used in agile development, it comprises three elements but for our purposes we think it is advisable to add a fourth outcome measurement clause and construct the user story in the following format.

As a [type of **user**],

    I want [some **goal**],

        so that [some **reason**],

            and I will know I am successful when I see [some **observable change in the situation**].

Notice the focus of the user story is not on the nuts and bolts of what the user is doing or what you need to do to serve them; the focus is very much on what they need to achieve, why they need to achieve it and how they will recognise that its achievement has instrumentally improved their situation. This is what we mean by outcome focus. User stories and a focus on your customers' needs and expectations will better equip you to see things from their perspective and keep you focused on critical outcomes.

Cultivate different styles of helping

When selecting people for customer-facing roles, the conventional wisdom is that you should value people with an empathetic disposition; people who listen carefully, try to understand and mirror behaviour and approach, and are capable of sympathising with the apparent situation. Everything tells us that this is the way forward, but perhaps this is not the whole story. Certainly, in low stress, collaborative situations this is a great personality profile, ideal for business analysts, but we have seen that the move to technology-mediated self-service has resulted in human contact being the last resort and frequently when the customer takes that option they have already reached a position of extreme frustration and argumentative helplessness. In such situations recent research (Dixon et al., 2017) suggests that the most effective and painless resolution is often provided by staff who take a 'controller' approach. Controllers tend to take over and drive the customer interaction; they can be opinionated and like to show off their expertise; they close rapidly on a solution and by doing so the key thing is that they are reducing the amount of customer effort that is required.

At every step of the way your aim is to reduce the customer effort in the transaction.

Controllers like to take charge of all situations and guide people. They tend to have strong personalities and make quick and confident decisions. In short, they display all the characteristics you don't normally associate with customer-facing roles and they are also the sort of people that you are least likely to hire into such a role. If your helpdesk and problem resolution section has a poor track record you would be well advised to put a couple of controllers into the mix.

In other, less stressful, customer interactions we suggest that you focus on the following key strategies.

- **Understand that different people engage differently,** so tailor your approach to the information processing and emotional needs of the customer.

- **Avoid channel switching.** What customers need is a gentle nudge towards the engagement channel that best suits their needs and preference for information access. One size does not fit all so you will need multiple channels, but giving people too many routes for engagement can also cause unnecessary confusion.

- **Accept the feedback you get from customers;** don't try to tell them it is easy when they have just told you it is not.

- **Use the feedback** from the disgruntled or struggling customers to point the way to reduce effort for all customers. If a customer is really vocal it is usually because they have had a particularly trying experience. By understanding how your systems and processes triggered and contributed to that frustration, you can gather important feedback that can help you reduce effort for everyone.

- **Focus management on producing low customer effort interactions** rather than trying to delight by giving them stuff they don't need or want.

THINGS FOR YOU TO WORK ON NOW

We have looked at a number of concepts in this chapter; the questions and exercises listed below will help you examine the practices of your team and assess how customer focused you are.

KEY QUESTIONS TO ASK YOURSELF

- When we engage with a customer or business partner, how much time and effort do we invest in really trying to understand their 'job to be done'?

- How easy is it to do business with my team (ETDBW)? When a customer or business partner engages with us how often do we switch channel or point of contact on them? Do we consciously try to guide our customer or business partner to an appropriate communication channel for them?

- Do I understand all the touch points in the journey for my key customers or business partners?

- Can we clearly articulate a 'user story' for our key customers or business partners?

- How often do I ask my key customers or business partners what is really important to them when dealing with my team? What do they need from this relationship now and how do they want to see it change in the future?

- How much of my time and energy is devoted to ensuring the smooth running of internal processes and how much time am I spending on externally facing activities that my customers or business partners would value and be prepared to pay for?

- As a team, is our focus on reacting to the symptoms our customers or business partners report so that we can get rid of them quickly and report the incident closed, or are we dedicated to exploring and solving the deeper issue in a way that improves the customers' or business partners' experience and makes their life easier?

- Do members of my team feel that they have the authority and autonomy to solve a customer's or business partner's problem when they see something going wrong or about to go wrong?

Reflect on your answers to the above questions and then try to build that new understanding into your everyday practice by trying the two thinking exercises listed below. Each of these exercises will give you a map or diagram that should help you to shape future conversations and become more customer focused in everything you do. All of this will result in you identifying, working on and developing:

- new behaviours that take the customers' view as prime;
- a new emphasis on what is important and a focus on outcomes;
- new ways of speaking and engaging at all levels of the business.

MINI EXERCISES YOU CAN TRY IMMEDIATELY

- Choose a key customer or business partner and map their 'customer journey': all the touch points that they have with your team as you initiate, complete and provide care for their requested product or service. Look at each touch point from the customer's perspective: What do they have to do in order to engage with you? What could you do to reduce the effort they have to make?

- Choose one of your key customers or business partners and express their needs as a 'user story'. How well do your team members understand and identify with the 'user story' for this customer? What can you all learn by looking at this customer from this perspective? Consider how your understanding of their desired outcomes has changed as a result of this process.

If you are inspired to find out more about any of the themes covered in this chapter we suggest that you start by reviewing the resources listed below.

FURTHER FOOD FOR THE CURIOUS

- Dixon, M., Freeman, K. and Toman, N. (2010) `Stop Trying to Delight Your Customers'. *Harvard Business Review*, July–August. Available from https://hbr.org/2010/07/stop-tryig-to-dlight-your-customers [3 November 2017]:

  - This article takes a different slant on customer service and moves the discussion to strategies that can help customers solve their problems. It introduces the idea of 'customer effort score', a measure of how easy it is for a customer to do business with you.

- Dixon, M., Ponomareff, L., Turner, S. and DeLisi, R. (2017) 'Kick-Ass Customer Service'. *Harvard Business Review*, January–February. Available from https://hbr.org/2017/01/kick-ass-customer-service [3 November 2017]:

  - An excellent article about their research conducted with customer service teams. It looks at seven different types of behavioural interaction patterns and much of this thinking is very relevant to any customer-facing IT role.

- Christensen, C.M., Cook, S. and Hall, T. (2005) 'Marketing Malpractice: The Cause and the Cure'. *Harvard Business Review*, December: 74–83:

  - Although the focus is on marketing and brand building, this article introduces the idea of the 'job to be done' and is an interesting read that contains many useful insights that are directly transferable into the IT domain and can help bridge the gap in the understanding between IT and the rest of the business.

2 SEEING THE BIG PICTURE AND THINKING STRATEGICALLY

The focus of this chapter is on how to develop and practise your capability as a strategic thinker. We distinguish core capabilities that mark out strategic thinking and stress the importance of making time in your diary to reflect and really think.

WHY IS THIS IMPORTANT?

Surveys show that **strategic thinking** is one of the top three capabilities that are valued and looked for in senior leaders. Most management competency frameworks include strategic thinking, so this is something that interviewers try to identify during the job selection process. However, it is one of the things that interview candidates have most difficulty understanding, discussing and giving practical examples that demonstrate their capability.

Organisations cannot survive by just aimlessly repeating what they did last year, or even last month. You need to be able to respond to changing circumstances, take advantage of emerging trends and constantly find new ways of delighting your customers with new levels of service and products that were previously unimaginable.

To this end, a fundamental capability for all managers is the ability to initiate and bring about change. But an organisation needs its change initiatives to be aligned towards a common purpose. That purpose is articulated in the business strategy and managers need to be able to internalise that strategy to the extent that it provides a guiding framework for all their decision-making.

THE IMPACT OF THE ISSUE

You may have seen organisations being torn apart by parochial decision-making that puts the narrow needs of a function above the broad goals of the organisation. All too often, you probably witness local decision-making that can only hope to serve the ends of local leadership.

Strategic thinkers are people who can think holistically and see beyond the limits of the current issue. They take a broad perspective on how a proposed course of action can contribute to the achievement of the long-term goals of an organisation as a whole, as well as resolving the immediate local problem.

When you are busy and stressed, and faced with a critical problem, it is difficult to find either the time or the perspective to see beyond the bounds of the immediate, but the strategic thinker always takes the broader perspective and the longer-term view.

The way you demonstrate strategic thinking is to focus on things that can contribute to bringing about long-term objectives. You should always use this perspective as the basis for your decision-making.

When you fix things with an eye to the long-term impacts or consequences they tend to stay fixed. On the other hand, if you make your decisions based solely on the impact in the here and now, the problems have a nasty habit of coming right back again.

Strategic thinking is not just the preserve of the leaders at the very top of the organisation. Organisations need all managers and leaders at all levels to think and act strategically; that means understanding how what you are doing contributes to the achievement of the long-term goals of your organisation. It means making connections between the ideas, initiatives and desired outcomes that your organisation is pursuing and ultimately having different sorts of conversations with the people who are involved in delivering elements of the strategy.

MAKING SENSE OF IT ALL

If you Google 'strategic thinking', you will get in excess of 8 million hits. If you take a little time to investigate some of the hits, you will quickly notice that the content is long on business strategy and the process of crafting winning strategies, and very short on explanation of the different sort of thinking that is needed.

It would appear that most experts think that strategic thinking is what you do in order to create a business strategy. But when you go for a job interview and the HR representative tells you that they really need someone who can think strategically, they are not saying they expect you to work up their business strategy – no, that's what the board does. So, that presents the following questions:

- What do they mean when they say they want a strategic thinker?

- What is strategic thinking and how is it different from the rest of the thinking you do?

- Does it need some elaborate process?

- Can it only be done when you are consciously formulating strategy?

An important skill of strategic thought is the ability to take a different view of a situation. But not just any different view; what you need is a view that allows you clear sight of your objective, where you are trying to get to, while at the same time letting you see the terrain that stands between you and your objective.

A good way to understand the nature of strategic thinking is to visualise the experience of walking a maze. As you enter a maze, you do so with no clear view of where you are trying to get to. You know you want to get to the middle, but you cannot see the middle and you have no idea where it is or how to get there. So, each time you come to a junction you are faced with having to make a choice; without any plan or overall route you can only make random choices. Each choice has the effect of opening or closing options but without any feedback on the success of the previous choice.

If, on the other hand, you were provided with a plan view of the maze taken from above, you would have no difficulty in seeing the most direct route to the centre. It seems obvious, but when you know what your objective is, and when you can see that objective in a broader context, decision-making becomes much easier and your route to success more sure and direct.

This is a great metaphor for strategic thinking. Sadly, though, many managers behave as if they are in a maze with no overall plan of what the maze or their objective looks like. Far too much organisational decision-making appears to be random, with no guidance from a consistent objective or set of guiding principles.

> Many of the managers we talk to get so wrapped up in dealing with the day-to-day stuff that lands on their desk and conscientiously dealing with every email they receive and attending every meeting they are invited to that 'they can't see the wood for the trees'. As a consequence, the business has moved on and IT ends up delivering to yesterday's need rather than the needs of tomorrow.

Most of the time, most of our thinking is what might be termed analytical and forward pass. You start with the problem and work forwards through logical steps until you find a potential solution. This form of thinking is so deeply ingrained in all of us through our education and experience that many people think that it is the only valid way to think, and that any other process is not real thinking.

But there is another way to think. Stephen Covey calls it 'backwards thinking' or 'beginning with the end in mind'; he sets this out in his *The 7 Habits of Highly Effective People* (2004). Others call it systems thinking, backward-pass thinking, intuition or synthesis. Whatever you call it, the process is as follows (see Figure 2.1):

Figure 2.1 Backward-pass thinking

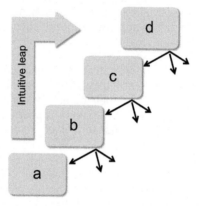

You make an intuitive leap from 'a' to an attractive, but as yet unrealised, outcome 'd'.

You then work backwards, asking yourselves, 'What do you need to put in place now to make this outcome more likely to come about in the future?'

The important thing to realise is that the future state 'd' does not yet exist, nor is there any certainty that it will ever exist.

The leap you make is not about predicting a future that will happen, but of imagining a future that you would find beneficial and then taking purposeful action now that you believe will increase the probability that your desired future will come about.

When you start to work backwards from 'd' you are not doing detailed planning of the steps you need to close the gap, but rather putting in place capabilities that make the realisation of this future more probable than the possible alternatives.

Strategic thinkers take steps to create the future rather than waiting for someone else's future to happen and then having to react to it.

Key to this sort of thinking is the recognition that you operate within complex, adaptive, self-organising systems and that a fundamental property of such systems is 'emergence'. New and unpredictable properties emerge as self-organising systems adapt to their environment.

So, the actions you put in place will have both intended and unintended consequences. A key skill is, therefore, to be alert to the emergence of new trends and to intelligently and opportunistically grasp these possibilities for the overall benefit of your organisations as a whole.

A venture capital company launched a project to provide access to their systems 'any time, any place, anywhere'; the initial estimate was, however, prohibitively expensive. Through his appreciation of 'up and coming' technologies, one of the most junior members of the team was able to suggest an alternative and significantly cheaper solution, one that ultimately won them an award for 'technical design and innovative use of technology'.

Strategy is not about blindly implementing some grand plan; it is about being aware of your environment. Looking for trends and unexpected or outlying readings that indicate that something fundamental may have changed. Things are constantly in flux and you need to be ready to recognise and exploit opportunities that emerge. You also need to do so in a way that is consistent with the overall aims of your business. If you accept this definition of strategic thinking, then the core skills that you need to develop are as follows:

- **Outcome-focused thinking:** being able to project yourself into the future and imagine a set of circumstances that would be beneficial for you or your organisation. You then need to craft a series of statements that describe the characteristics of that future's state in terms of the capabilities you would need to create it and what it would feel like once you got there. Key to this is the ability to see every situation in its wider context.

- **Backward-pass thinking:** having imagined a desirable future, constantly ask questions such as: What would you need to put in place to make this happen?

- **Intelligent opportunism:** being alert to emerging trends and taking advantage of them.

To complete the process of strategic thinking, ultimate decision-making needs to be grounded in a set of core principles that place a higher value on promoting action to realise the desired outcomes than on merely taking action to resolve the symptoms of the problem that you are faced with.

PRACTICAL ADVICE

A key purpose of strategy is to produce action that is aligned towards a compelling long-term goal. So, as well as being able to think strategically you need to be able to communicate strategically; that means using language in a way that engages both hearts and minds and inspires people towards a consistent set of actions and choices. Most technical people are very good at talking in detailed terms but not so skilled at painting a vivid picture of a situation that drives a sense of purpose. The good news is that you don't need to be engaged in strategy making to practise the skills you need for using strategic language. We suggest that you practise the following exercises as a way of polishing your outcome-focused view of a situation. All of these skills will improve with deliberate practise and appropriate feedback. Trying these techniques should not be a one-time effort on your part; you need to come back to them repeatedly over time, focusing on improving key aspects of your performance:

First, write a summary of a book or article that you have just read. Your summary should be no more than a single page of A4. This will require you to identify the governing thought of the book: what is the key message that everyone should take from reading this book?

Second, next time you visit a new city, imagine that you have been asked to write one paragraph for a travel brochure giving the potential visitor an impression of what they might experience. Again, the key to this task lies not in descriptive detail, but rather in your ability to discern a unique characteristic of a city and to convey that in a compelling manner, so that others might be captivated by the impressions you have conveyed. Your message needs to be emotionally compelling, but anchored in an achievable reality.

Having honed your language skills you need to proactively make time for thinking and that means really sensing what is going on both inside your organisation and in the wider industry sector. What trends do you see and what does not fit? To get better at backward-pass thinking, try to incorporate some of the following ideas into the way you analyse what you see:

- First, start with the visionary purpose: what do you want things to look like at some point in the future?

This can be as far-fetched as you like; in fact, the wackier the better.

- Next, list and quantify the benefits you are seeking by creating this future.

- Then, consider which parts of the organisation will be involved in delivering the identified benefits.

- Finally, identify the capabilities that would need to be in place to bring about this environment and outcomes that you could create.

- Now you may refine your visionary purpose into something that would sound more potentially realistic.

- Think about the way you spend your time. How much of your daily time is devoted to activities that are directed towards the realisation of the capabilities that you have just imagined? What can you stop doing that will free up more of your time to think and act in a way that contributes to the achievement of these outcomes?

As your environment does not remain static, you also need to attune yourself to spot emergent factors and behave with intelligent opportunism. Try the following techniques:

- Paint a vision for your industry in five years' time.

- Consider the generic technological capabilities that exist today, and consider how you could harness them to the advantage of your organisation.

- Consider examples of competitive advantage gained in other industries. What are the common themes? How could any of these be applied to your industry?

- Always remember to think of the possibilities rather than the problems. Reflect on the famous quote attributed to Thomas Edison: 'I did not fail: I just succeeded in finding 100 ways not to make a light bulb'.

You might want to repeat the above exercise but with different time horizons. Notice how as you move further into the future you naturally engage in more 'blue sky' thinking. What would it take to bring ideas from your 20 year horizon into the reality of today? Now that you are on your way to developing the three core skills of strategic thinking, you need to align your decision-making around the core principles of achieving the desired outcomes and focusing on root causes rather than symptoms. You will know that you have succeeded in this when:

- you are leading the way rather than following or copying that of a competitor;
- you have provided direction and inspiration rather than prescription and rigidity;
- the people around you are excited by possibilities and choices;
- there is a positive atmosphere and people feel liberated rather than constrained;
- things are starting to happen and change for the better.

THINGS FOR YOU TO WORK ON NOW

Strategic thinking is not something you do once a year; it should be a normal part of the way you think about your contribution to achieving business outcomes. We have pointed to key skills that you need to develop that will help you to think, act and communicate in a way that marks you out as someone who understands and contributes to the wider goals of the organisation. Before you start to practise these skills, you need to make an honest appraisal of how you currently operate. Try asking yourself the following questions.

KEY QUESTIONS TO ASK YOURSELF

- What is the most radical or wacky idea that I have ever had?

- How comfortable am I with taking risks?

- How much do I rely upon past experience, the tried and tested, or best practice?

- How comfortable am I with ambiguity, uncertainty and complexity?

- How prepared am I to put my neck on the line for what I believe in?

- How prepared am I to follow my gut instinct, or what my heart tells me?

- How much time do I dedicate to 'strategic thinking'? If I am honest with myself, do I prefer to focus on day-to-day issues?

- How often do I make time to reflect on what is happening?

- How much do I encourage my team members to reflect on their contribution and talk about trends that they are seeing in our internal environment?

Think about your answers to the above questions and now work on the exercises suggested below. This is not a one-off activity; we suggest you revisit these exercises several times over the coming weeks and use them to practise your strategic conversations.

MINI EXERCISES YOU CAN TRY IMMEDIATELY

- Write down the strategic direction of your organisation in one simple, easy-to-understand sentence.

- Within the context of the strategic direction of your organisation, write down your purpose, again in one simple and easy-to-understand sentence.

- Within the context of the above, think of three initiatives that would make a difference to your organisation for the better – be opportunistic; be off the wall. These may only be small initiatives, but they are all that is needed at this stage, as long as they fulfil all the other criteria.

FURTHER FOOD FOR THE CURIOUS

- Bowman, N. (2016) '4 Ways to Improve Your Strategic Thinking Skills'. *Harvard Business Review*, December. Available from https://hbr.org/2016/12/4-ways-to-improve-your-strategic-thinking-skills [3 November 2017]:

  - A concise and compelling digital article that gives some valuable practical advice.

- Davey, L. (2014) 'Strengthen Your Strategic Thinking Muscles'. *Harvard Business Review*, January. Available from https://hbr.org/2014/01/strengthen-your-strategic-thinking-muscles [3 November 2017]:

  - A two-page digital article that stresses the importance of making time for reflection and strategy as willingness to make choices about what you do and do not do.

- Collins, J. (2005) 'Level 5 Leadership: The Triumph of Humility and Fierce Resolve'. *Harvard Business Review*, July–August. Available from https://hbr.org/2005/07/level-5-leadership-the-triumph-of-humility-and-fierce-resolve [3 November 2017]:

  - An excellent article about their research into what catapults a company from merely good to truly great.

- Covey, S.R. (2004) *The 7 Habits of Highly Effective People*: *Powerful Lessons in Personal Change*. Simon & Schuster, London:
  - An excellent insight into the process of strategic thinking and what makes one person highly effective in their role.

3 SEEING NEW OPPORTUNITIES AND RECOGNISING THE UNEXPECTED BEFORE IT HAPPENS

The focus of this chapter is on increasing your powers of perception; you do this by learning to see differently. All the evidence suggests that people who appear to have the ability to anticipate events are really just more sensitive to spotting unusual indicators, seeing things that you have trained your brain to ignore.

WHY IS THIS IMPORTANT?

Try to remember when you first learned to drive a car. Quite apart from the fact that you certainly drove a lot more slowly, we can guarantee that, as you looked out of the windscreen, your point of focus was just beyond the end of the bonnet – maybe 10 to 15 metres ahead.

In all probability, your mind was telling you that the main perils lay immediately ahead of you and were already in your path. Later on, as an experienced driver, your focus probably shifted to 100 to 150 metres ahead. You learned not to watch the brake lights of the car ahead, but to look instead at the reflection of the brake lights of the car three cars ahead.

This shift of focus brought about a shift of behaviour. You started to look for things that were developing, or could develop, into dangers, rather than just reacting to things that had already become life-threatening.

As you become more experienced, you find that you can anticipate what is likely to happen based on patterns of activity that you have experienced before. Also, you continually, and subconsciously, store up new patterns and, consequently, become even more adept at recognising danger before it arises.

Yes, there is the odd moron who sits in their air-conditioned cocoon, totally oblivious of all other road users, but most of us have evolved beyond that. We all have the innate capacity to look ahead, anticipate potential futures and take appropriate action.

If you can do it in the fast-paced and potentially lethal area of car driving, why do you find it so difficult to do it at work?

THE IMPACT OF THE ISSUE

Our organisations are full of people running around like headless chickens, locked into an endless cycle of meetings. They are always reacting to the latest crisis, forever busy, but never having time to actually do anything.

Leaders often moan that they need to be more proactive and less reactive, and then scream at you about the latest set of critical business service availability figures. Being proactive isn't just a catchy new-age management fad; it is your route to salvation and sanity.

Learning to look outwards and upwards is the key to seeing problems before they become major crises.

Crisis situations throw you into reactive fire-fighting mode, dealing with the fallout and limiting the damage. They negatively impact productivity and morale, sap your energy and increase your stress levels.

We have always marvelled when watching Roger Federer at his peak, playing in the finals at Wimbledon. He appeared to read the game so well that he had the ability to always be in the right place at just the right time; consequently, he never appeared to be moving very quickly or to be rushed into any manoeuvre. That is the sign of greatness.

The greats always have time to exceed expectations with time and energy to spare; they remain unruffled, have reserves of energy and make things look easy. They are not superhuman. Yes, they may be exceptionally talented, they may have developed levels of technical prowess previously unseen, but in all cases what they share is two key skills: (i) they are better at anticipating events than the people around them; and (ii) they don't wait passively for the future to happen to them, they take actions now that make it more likely that an advantageous future will come about.

The ability to anticipate is rooted in the ability to read events as they are emerging.

The good news is that all of us are capable of anticipating possible future events and it is a capability that can be learned and refined. Once we learn to read events we are better placed to make decisions that shape those events to our advantage.

MAKING SENSE OF IT ALL

We live in a world of seemingly unlimited information. In the past, most of us have experienced data overload occasionally. Now, and in the future, it is likely to be a permanent state of being.

The good news is that our brains are naturally wired to protect us from data overload. The bad news is that they do this by filtering out what doesn't appear to be immediately relevant.

Of course, our brain's idea of relevance is based on what it has seen before. We look just long enough for our brain to recognise a pattern; then it says, 'Oh, I know what this is, it's an example of ...'; and then we stop looking.

To help us make more sense of the world and gain greater insight from the phenomena that are there for us to observe we will explore three key concepts:

- recognising new patterns;
- developing future memories;
- extending our experience across boundaries.

Recognising new patterns

The first step to seeing new opportunities and recognising unexpected future outcomes is to learn to increase your ability to recognise new patterns; in effect, you first need to learn to see anew.

If you accept that your brain works on pattern recognition then the only way to increase your powers of perception is to increase the number of patterns that your brain uses to find a match. You need to work on constantly exposing your brain to new experiences and new sensations, and, at the same time, ask yourself new and different questions about the experiences that you are having.

Young children do this naturally. Everything is new to them and everything new is associated with a barrage of inquiring questions: 'Why does that do that? What would happen if? Why have I not got one of ...? Where did this come from? Who made ...? Where does this go at night?' Sadly, as we grow older, we lose our sense of wonder; we stop asking daft questions; and we start to limit our range of experiences by actively repeating only those things that have worked for us or pleased us in the past. In effect, our past becomes the limiting factor on our potential future.

Time and time again in IT we make the same mistakes. We think we know the answer; we think we know best; we believe we are more intelligent so we don't ask the question or check our facts. Instead we make an assumption which in hindsight turns out to be fundamentally flawed. We know we do it; we know we are likely to do it in the future; and yet we keep on doing it. Indeed, we both confess to falling into this trap ourselves.

Developing future memories

Second, you need to become a little more conscious about how your brain works and what it does with stuff. Current thinking about how the brain works suggests that it stores experiences as patterns (or, if you prefer, memories). The interesting thing is that it appears to make no differentiation between patterns of events that you have actually experienced and events that you have just mentally rehearsed.

This is an intriguing idea and has caused some neuroscientists to call this process creating **memories of the future**.[4] This idea underpins organisational approaches such as scenario planning. This is a process where you pose apparently unlikely questions and mentally grapple with (rehearse) how you might react if these events occurred. In doing so, the argument is that the brain now stores patterns of these events, as if you had actually experienced them.

Amazingly, although the events have not actually happened, the fact that you have thought about them is enough to store them away. You are, therefore, more likely to perceive them and attach relevance to them in the event that you observe one or more of the symptoms or indicators that they may be happening. You are, in effect, storing memories of possible futures.

---

[4] Ingvar D.H. (1985) 'Memory of the Future': An Essay on the Temporal Organisation of the Conscious Awareness.

By storing more patterns in your brain, you are increasing the likelihood that you will attach significance to an event or happening that you would otherwise have ignored. You will develop the capacity to recognise the potential significance of things that your colleagues are ignoring.

When conducting post-implementation reviews I (Robina) frequently uncover all the warning signs and bells that things are starting to go wrong. These, however, are generally ignored. The situation only becomes evident when it has reached crisis point. The signs are sometimes subtle – for example, body language not matching words – but are often more obvious such as a key stakeholder asking for reassurance that something won't go wrong or that something else will be included.

Extending our experiences across boundaries

The third element of our journey to increased understanding is learning to stand in the shoes of others. So, in addition to taking steps to increase your own range of experiences, you can also try to tap into how other people might experience the same, or similar, circumstances. In effect, you need to take every opportunity you can to experience the world through the eyes of others.

Researchers in the field of organisational development and innovation management are now calling this capacity '**boundary spanning**' – stepping across the artificial boundaries of organisational or social structures to experience the world as others see it. In her groundbreaking book, *Hot Spots: Why Some Companies Buzz with Energy and Innovation and Others Don't* (2007), the London Business School professor Lynda Gratton identified boundary spanning as a key enabler of innovation.

It turns out that boundary spanning is one of the most important factors in increasing the innovative capacity of an organisation. When you engage with people from different departments, different companies, different industries and different cultures, you start to see and experience different aspects of a situation. When you are unhampered by the limitations of past experience, you can start to see dimensions of potential solutions that would otherwise be hidden from you.

Other people see things differently and, therefore, can see different solutions to problems that you have found to be intractable. As you increase your exposure to these alternative ways of seeing and being, you also increase your ability to sense triggers in your environment that can alert you to things before they happen. In effect, you are increasing your ability to anticipate events before they hit you.

A century ago Gaudi's architecture took inspiration from nature. Today, engineers are also looking towards nature for inspiration; two examples are the FlexShapeGripper, which can pick up and place objects of diverse shapes in a single process and owes its existence to the chameleon's tongue; also we see intelligent bionic ants co-operating to move large and awkward objects.

The web has also provided the means for organisations to gain access to bright and willing workers anywhere in the world. An example is the website MindSumo. com. This connects young students in universities and colleges to corporate businesses who post their problems as challenges with cash prizes for great solutions. The evidence so far appears to suggest that the most innovative solutions tend to come from students studying in subject areas that would not normally be associated with the nature of the challenge.

So, in summary, there are three key skills associated with being able to anticipate the unexpected and recognise new opportunities:

- Get better at seeing things that are currently within your sphere of activity, but that you are unaware of, or you are in the practice of ignoring.

- Expose yourself to more potential patterns by mentally rehearsing how you would react to plausible but unlikely scenarios.

- Broaden your general ability to perceive by learning to see through the eyes of others.

PRACTICAL ADVICE

You have seen that if you can populate your brain with more experiences and hence more patterns, you will increase the chance of your brain finding relevance in the indicators in the environment and, hence, you increase your powers of perception.

Try doing some of the following things:

- Find opportunities to spend time working in other departments and look to rotate your staff through various roles and departments.

- Volunteer to serve on cross-functional initiatives, whole-organisation changes and so on.

- Take an interest in what other departments are doing and try to understand the values that underpin their initiatives.

- Understand the end-to-end nature of the processes that your department is engaged in. Where do the inputs come from? Where do your outputs go and how are they used? Think along the time line as well as the process flow.

- When you have a particularly challenging problem, try to simulate the various alternative solutions. You can do this by:

  - role play;
  - structured walk-throughs;

- problem brainstorming sessions – if you do this, make sure you have a wide range of experience and backgrounds in the group;
- computer simulations.

- If your industry is changing, or facing new competitors, try using the techniques of scenario planning. Develop a range of questions that challenge the basic assumptions of your industry and then work through these questions in a mixed group.

- Stand back and ask the big questions 'What is the purpose of this?' and 'Why do we do it this way?' or even 'What would happen if we didn't do it at all?'

You have also seen that putting yourself in the shoes of others is a key way of seeing differently. Try to build some of the following boundary-spanning activities into your routine:

- Get into the habit of having lunch or coffee with people from different professions, different disciplines or different departments from you.

- Keep a whiteboard in your office and get into the habit of talking through perplexing problems with your staff and maybe even visitors. Use visualisation and mapping techniques to build up images of potential solutions. A sort of soft requirements engineering.

- Attend conferences on topics that attract people from different industries or professions. Use the opportunity to network; talk to them and make lasting connections. Don't waste this valuable opportunity by spending the time checking your email and catching up with the issues of the day back at the ranch.

- Increase the breadth of your reading. If you are a software engineer, try reading some popular literature explaining developments in biotechnology, genetics or finance.

- Read eclectic journals, such as *Harvard Business Review*, *Nature*, *The Economist* and *Fast Company*.

- Take up a new hobby, one that is likely to expose you to different cultures and ways of thinking. For example, if you are a programmer, try your hand at amateur dramatics.

- Consider some form of higher education, but do it in a discipline where you have no experience. For instance, if you have a background in information security, go and study the history of art, or something so different that it will give you a whole new perspective.

THINGS FOR YOU TO WORK ON NOW

The first step to being able to see the unexpected is to train your brain by feeding it as many real or mentally rehearsed experiences as possible.

Below are some questions that will help you conduct a personal audit of your current level of forward thinking and boundary spanning.

KEY QUESTIONS TO ASK YOURSELF

- What is your horizon? How often and how far do you think ahead? How much of your time is spent dealing with day-to-day issues versus planning or developing yourself for the future?

- When did you last take a whole day out for thinking about the future or scenario planning?

- When you attend a conference or training course, can you tear yourself away from your email and make the most of the opportunity to meet people, make new connections and 'boundary span'?

- How often do you connect with people from other departments; other organisations; other disciplines; other industry sectors?

- When was the last time you encouraged your team to think about how they would react to the development of a situation that you all think is very unlikely or even improbable?

- Do you have a vision for your department in, say, five years' time?

- Do you know where your company is headed? Could you readily articulate your company's vision and strategy for the future?

The above questions will give you some insight into how effective you currently are at seeing and thinking about the unusual and how often you engage with people who see the world very differently from yourself. Below are some practical steps that you can take to expand your powers of perception.

MINI EXERCISES YOU CAN TRY IMMEDIATELY

- Next time you attend a conference, or training course, set up an 'out-of-office' reply and take an email vacation. Your organisation will not collapse in a heap without you. Maximise the opportunity and spend every waking minute of your time networking and building 'boundary-spanning' relationships for the future.

- Plan, each week, to have lunch or coffee with someone from a different area within your organisation.

- Each month, take a whole day out to consider the future: What will you be doing? How will your department be organised? What new processes will there need to be in, say, three years' time?

- Paint a mental picture of your industry sector in five years' time.

FURTHER FOOD FOR THE CURIOUS

- Bhasker, M. (2016) *Curation: The Power of Selection in a World of Excess*. Piatkus Press, London:

  - A wide-ranging book that takes a new look at information overload and suggests that the route to creating value is through careful curation of resources.

- Day, G.S. and Schoemaker, P.J.H. (2006) *Peripheral Vision: Detecting the Weak Signals that Will Make or Break Your Company*. Harvard Business School Press, Boston, MA:

  - A landmark book that shows how and why organisations fail to see important signals that could indicate disruptive change.

- Hayashi, A.M. (2001) 'When to Trust Your Gut'. *Harvard Business Review*, February. Available from https://hbr.org/2001/02/when-to-trust-your-gut [3 November 2017]:

  - A short, yet excellent, article that provides examples of 'out-of-the-box' thinking and practical advice on to how to sharpen your intuition.

4 BUILDING A SPIRIT OF INNOVATION

The focus of this chapter is helping people to find solutions to their most intractable problems by asking different questions, finding ways to really share and value all ideas and looking for solutions in unexpected places. As a team leader, you need to inspire your team to plug their existing knowledge together in ways that produce breakthrough possibilities. When you are faced with a gap in your knowledge you will commonly seek the assistance of someone more experienced who works in exactly the same domain as yourself, but often the greatest insight can be found from people who, at first glance, don't appear to be anything like you or engaged in the same endeavours as you are.[5] This chapter will show you ways in which you can start to tap into wells of much greater knowledge and insight.

WHY IS THIS IMPORTANT?

It is common to presume that innovation is always the result of a bright idea and that such bright ideas only occur inside the heads of seriously clever people, people who are not in any way like us, people who are collected together in a special department, often called 'research and development'.

Nothing could be further from the truth. Increasingly, we see innovation not as something that occurs inside the heads of

---

[5] Many great innovations came about by adapting or building upon ideas from one industry to solve problems in another. For a range of great examples of this phenomenon see Ramon Vullings and Marc Heleven's book *Not Invented Here: Cross-industry Innovation* (2015).

smart people, but rather as something that happens in the spaces between inquisitive people.

> What really makes innovation work is connecting people, especially people who think differently and have different skills and experience.

Innovation is not the same as creativity; the focus is not on conjuring up something amazing out of nothing, but rather on finding new ways of plugging together existing knowledge to deliver new and exciting outcomes.

We often hear people say 'Oh, I'm not a creative person', or 'I'm no good at thinking strategically', or 'I've never had an original idea'. The manager's job is to help people to rise above such self-limiting statements of personal inadequacy. We are all innovators in our own way, and when we engage constructively with people who see the world in a slightly different light from ourselves, we open up the possibility of producing great new insights and new ways of working.

THE IMPACT OF THE ISSUE

Our organisations face many challenges: doing more with fewer resources, changing demographics, skills shortages, environmental pressures, evolving legislative structures and financial pressures, to name but a few. One thing is for sure, doing more of the same, or just focusing on getting better at what you can already do well, is not a sustainable model. This is not a new phenomenon and is captured nicely by one of the greatest thinkers of our time:

> The significant problems that we face cannot be solved with the same level of thinking that created them. (Albert Einstein)

Or, to put it in the form of a mantra increasingly popular with senior leaders:

> If you always do what you always did, you will always get what you always got. (Henry Ford)

> Innovation is about finding combinations of new and existing insights that generate new possibilities for our customers to fulfil their 'jobs to be done'.

MAKING SENSE OF IT ALL

Being great at innovation is not a matter of luck. Organisations and teams that are good at innovating tend to have a characteristic culture, a culture that values constructive questioning, healthy co-operation and an openness to new experiences and ways of thinking. Innovations are most likely to happen when a team has:

- **A shared purpose** that inspires them and ignites action. Interestingly, such a purpose is seldom created as a result of a top-down edict; it comes through curiosity, questioning and challenging each other to achieve something special.

- **A willingness to truly co-operate**, to give freely of personal resources to help others to develop and test their ideas. This requires an emphasis on the greater good, rather than on local or short-term gains, and it involves collaboration and a preparedness to compromise on individual interests in order to achieve the best overall result.

- **An openness to engage with people** who think and see the world differently. You will often ignore things that are right in front of your eyes because you have long considered them to be irrelevant, but someone new to a situation sees everything for the first time and sees with a mind that has different values and experiences.

A relatively young Luxembourg-based bank offered investment products to high-net-worth individuals. Over time they had introduced more and more checks and balances, meaning that a new customer would now not receive interest on their investment for seven days after deposit – this led to some very unhappy customers. Tom, a newly appointed business relationship manager, together with a stranger met by chance while waiting for a delayed flight, together came up with a revolutionary solution: the company took out an insurance policy to mitigate any risk of mistake and could therefore revert back to the one day processing times it originally offered for new deposits.

You will increase your chance of seeing anew when you cross organisational or industry boundaries – innovations nearly always come by applying something from one field or scientific discipline to another field or scientific discipline. People who can span boundaries are critical to increasing innovation.

Innovation also needs to be managed differently from business as usual. In business as usual, the emphasis has to be on right first time and every time. However, in order to innovate you must experiment and when you experiment you must expect to fail. So, managing for an innovative culture means that you must strive for ultimate success while embracing the possibility of many small failures along the way. You should embrace those failures and view them as a learning opportunity.

IT people frequently strive to perfect what they already know. By contrast, innovation usually involves grappling with unknown quantities and unpredictable consequences; under these circumstances, hitting the jackpot first time is unlikely and perfection is well downstream.

For innovation to thrive, you need to cultivate a culture that values people who try, however imperfectly, to seize the unknown. Figure 4.1 depicts the three pillars of an innovative culture built upon the solid foundations of a highly tuned productive capacity.

Figure 4.1 Three pillars of capability

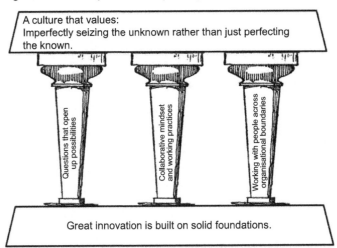

A culture that values:
Imperfectly seizing the unknown rather than just perfecting the known.

Questions that open up possibilities

Collaborative mindset and working practices

Working with people across organisational boundaries

Great innovation is built on solid foundations.

The three core capabilities that underpin innovation are:

- **Questions that open up possibilities.** Every innovation starts with a question, and the very best innovations emerge when you ask questions that challenge conventional wisdom and open the possibility of being different. The problem is that, most of the time, most of us are not very good at asking questions. Or, when we do ask questions, we use our questions as a weapon to put people down rather than as a mechanism to lift people up. Consider the following points:

    - Research shows[6] that poorly performing teams tend to ask 1 question for every 20 statements. High-performing teams have a ratio much closer to 1 to 1.

---

[6] Marcial Losada and Emily Heaphy in 2004 conducted one of the most comprehensive studies on the role of connectivity in the performance of business teams (The Role of Positivity and Connectivity in the Performance of Business Teams.

- A good question can act as an igniting catalyst for a team and challenge and inspire them; a bad question can debilitate them and freeze them into inactivity.

- The best questions are future-focused and challenge existing thinking, collective wisdom and organisational or industry paradigms; they may shake deeply held personal values or beliefs.

A new CIO took over an IT function with a poor reputation that wasn't seen to 'deliver value for money' or 'understand and act on business priorities'. The new CIO dared to ask the question, 'What if we could become a profit centre – imagine the impact that could have on our standing within the organisation?' With the support and encouragement of her team, the new CIO drew up a marketing plan focusing on their multi-language capability that was to become their USP (unique selling point). Six months down the road saw a turnaround in IT's reputation and a small, but significant, contribution to the bottom line of the organisation.

- **Collaborative mindset and working practices.** To collaborate means to work with others on a joint project. To co-operate means to be of assistance or willing to assist. In order to stimulate innovation, collaboration has to be much more than just working together; it must embrace a sense of shared purpose, mutual responsibility and commitment to achieve win–win outcomes. Too much of our organisational behaviour is based on advocacy – this leads to a feeling that in order to win, others must lose. Being collaborative doesn't mean going with the flow or being unwilling to challenge what is expected. Collaboration works best when you listen respectfully, value and build on the ideas of others, and be willing to back winning ideas even when to do so may require personal courage and commitment. You show your desire to collaborate when you start using the word 'and', rather than the word 'but', when discussing new ideas. People collaborate most effectively when there is a common work product and a shared pride in the outcome. You need to be willing and prepared to volunteer and to give of your own scarce resources for the good of someone else's idea.

A manufacturing company had an unofficial strike on its hands and wanted to pay those in work but not those on strike. As a consequence, it couldn't run the normal payroll system, which would pay everyone. A team was formed comprising representatives from payroll, IT development, IT operations and the various manufacturing departments. They worked hard for long hours; there was lots of good humoured banter; and agile methods were deployed. Everyone was willing to share knowledge and everyone was willing to compromise their needs in order to meet the pay deadline. Within three days they had developed a very crude but operational payroll system.

- **Working with people across organisational boundaries.** The world's truly great innovations usually came about when people suddenly found a new way of seeing something that had always been there in front of them. You may see something being used for one purpose and start to ask the question of how that idea could be adapted to serve a completely different purpose. In order to increase the probability of this sort of breakthrough, you need to increase the amount of time that you spend with people who have a totally different experience from your own, and therefore interpret situations differently and see the world with different eyes. In short, you need to get out of your comfort zone and spend less time surrounded by people who think and act just like you. Think about the following two observations. First, a great organisational paradox is that breakthrough innovations and novel combinations are most likely to occur when you put people together who bring ideas from different sectors or disciplines. Yet organisations group similar people together, so that they are surrounded by people who think and act just like them. Second, people who see or experience something for the first time are likely to ask apparently facile questions that lead to great new insights.

A small butcher based in north London had been adversely affected by the arrival of a supermarket. As it was difficult to compete on price, the owner sought a different solution. As a result of a conversation with some 'tech' guys he met in his local pub one lunchtime, he fitted inexpensive sensors inside the store window to monitor pedestrian footfall via people's mobile phones. The findings proved the busiest time outside the shop was between 9 p.m. and midnight, when passers-by were heading to, or leaving, the two nearby pubs.

Using Google Trends, a free online tool, the owner investigated what the most popular food searches were and decided to open for a few hours in the evening selling pulled pork burgers and premium hot dogs. Now a significant chunk of his revenue comes from this small opening slot and his profit margins are much higher; in addition, he is using up meat that, in the past, would have gone to waste.

Too often people ignore insights from passing acquaintances or those lower down the organisational totem pole, or from others without their knowledge or with fewer qualifications.

Insight can, and does, come from anywhere – great innovators are constantly looking for different perspectives 'any time, any place, anywhere'.

PRACTICAL ADVICE

We will split our practical advice into three sections to reflect the three distinct capabilities that are so important for stimulating innovation. Let's start with ways to stimulate questions that open up possibilities:

1. Think of questions as a way to kick-start thinking and learning. Ask open, non-leading questions and phrase them in the future tense. Look for questions that challenge deeply held beliefs.

2. Rather than telling people what to do, try describing an outcome that you would like to achieve and then ask questions like:
   a. What would it feel like to work in that kind of environment?
   b. If we had this in place, what would we be able to do that we can't do now?
   c. What do we need to put in place now to start moving in this direction?
   d. What can you do individually that could support us all in this change?

3. Ask your team what one thing they could do that would transform the service they give to their customers:[7]

   a. Get your team to prioritise the ideas.
   b. Get them to work up some of the ideas into a practicable proposal.
   c. Get them to vote on which of the ideas are the most likely to be successful.
   d. See if you can start an experiment to check out the validity of the most popular idea – see how many people are prepared to invest some of their own spare time on the project.

---

[7] Some staff may come from a culture or environment where they were not expected or allowed to put forward ideas and this can make them reluctant to share their thoughts. In such cases trust and continual encouragement need to be built up over time through inclusion, active listening, positive feedback and respect.

e.   Once you have a working hypothesis, get the team to present it to management and see if you can get funding to take it further. Treat it like making a pitch to the bank manager for funding to start a new business.

Now let's look at some things you can do to create or support a collaborative mindset and collaborative working practices. The first thing to realise is that stimulating collaboration starts with your recruitment and induction processes.

Recruiting – When recruiting, we tend to look for people who can do the things we do and appear to be enthusiastic about how we do it. We are attracted to people who think like we do and hold similar values to ourselves. The problem with this is that we run the risk of hiring a bunch of people just like us; this is commonly referred to as the 'comfortable clone syndrome'. When we recruit, we have an opportunity to bring in fresh ideas and new thinking, so actively look for:

- people who ask you why you do things the way you do and look unimpressed when you explain why;

- people who have a passion for something and are looking for an opportunity to try it out in your company;

- people who ask you challenging questions during the interview; if they are confident enough to question you in an interview situation, the chances are they will continue to question you and everything once they are on the team. People who ask constructive questions are worth their weight in gold.

Induction processes – Our induction processes tend to focus on getting people to understand our processes, systems, values and beliefs. The idea is that the quicker we can get people to be just like us, the better. Actually, while we want new recruits to understand what we are trying to achieve, we should be slightly more wary about indoctrinating them into our ways, especially when a key element of their role is to be innovative in the solutions they produce. Try some of the following:

- Don't be too concerned if people appear to be slow at learning your processes or reluctant to embrace your ways. Instead of pushing harder to make them conform, ask them questions to understand their concerns and reservations.

- Focus on introducing new team members to peers who have a track record of questioning and producing good ideas.

- After two to three weeks, ask your new people what one process or practice they find most frustrating and why. Allow them to suggest better ways to achieve the same objectives. Get them to run a short workshop with a handful of your best thinkers to discuss the process or practice and how it could be better.

- Try to create a peer-to-peer network that spans all sections of the business and arrange regular meetings and encourage people to freely discuss the issues they are facing. Try to get informal groups to work together to develop and test new ideas in action.

Collaboration – Collaboration is not about meekly doing what you are asked to do and joining in. It is about volunteering for a task because you are inspired by the possibility of producing a new level of service or a previously unimagined product. Before people can volunteer, they need to know what is going on and they need to be engaged. Try some of the following ideas:

- Create an intranet site or collaboration space (this could be a physical space like a white board or office wall) where your team members can post their ideas, ideally anonymously. Build in a mechanism for the team to expand upon or supplement ideas or even suggest ways in which they could be developed into products or services. Establish a process where they can vote for the ideas they think are the best.

- Allow your team members to volunteer their services to develop the ideas that are top of the list.

- Encourage your team members to always ask 'Why?'

Finally, let's look at some of the things you can do to stimulate working across organisational boundaries and bringing ideas in from the outside:

- Get some magazines and journals from completely different disciplines – if you are a software developer, perhaps you could get professional journals on medicine, the biotech industry, oil exploration, toys and gaming, furniture design, geology, photography and so on. Encourage your team members to look through the articles and each month organise a 30-minute discussion around the article that people found most fascinating. Get them to work up three things that made this story so compelling; then challenge them to think of ways in which you could apply similar insight to your own industry.

- Arrange a short-term transfer for one of your team into a completely different role in another part of the organisation. When they come back, get them to brief your team on their experience. Suggest that they focus most on:

  - How are the people in the other role different?

  - What are their main priorities?

  - What are the big assumptions that appear to underpin their decision-making?

  - What do they worry about most?

  - What do they consider to be their biggest success in the last 12 months and why are they so proud of it?

  - What three things do they do that our team should try to copy?

  - What three things do they do that our team should try to avoid doing ourselves?

- Find opportunities for you to visit different industries and see how they do things. Think of it as a benchmarking exercise where the aim is to see how people work collaboratively, rather than trying to copy their process. Focus on the following areas:

- How does someone with a good idea bring it to the attention of the management?

- What percentage of the ideas that they are working on came from outside their organisation (a process increasingly known as open innovation)?

- When they have a problem they can't solve, how do they look for potential solution providers? Some organisations call this process scouting, i.e. looking for third-party providers who can bring new insight to an existing problem.

- What is their process for assessing the potential value of new ideas?

- Who decides who works on the key projects? What potential is there for people to volunteer their services or get involved with things that interest them?

THINGS FOR YOU TO WORK ON NOW

A strong focus of this chapter has been expanding your powers of perception by asking different questions and truly valuing ideas that come from external sources. Start by using the questions below to conduct an audit of how open you currently are to gathering external ideas. And once you have found new knowledge, how open are you to sharing and working collaboratively and how well do you model behaviours that encourage sharing and experimentation?

KEY QUESTIONS TO ASK YOURSELF

- What structures do you have in place to help members of your team engage with people from different departments, industries or professions?

- How many ideas come from outside your immediate team?

- How can you encourage people who don't work for you to contribute towards solving your problems or producing new ideas?

- How can you create a mechanism where team members have an element of choice about which projects to invest their personal resources in?

- Is it feasible for you to create an internal open market for ideas, where your team members can vote for those ideas that they feel are the biggest winners?

- How do people interact with each other within your organisation? Is their approach more competitive or more collaborative?

- What is the attitude of your organisation towards failure?

- How easily could you articulate your current 'shared purpose'?

Now use the techniques we have discussed to start to plan how you will manage the performance of your team differently. We suggest you start by focusing on the effect of your own language, specifically the way you frame challenges and the questions you ask of yourself and of your team. Your focus should be to use questions as a way of liberating your team to think rather than using questions as a weapon that drives people into their shells for fear of failing or looking stupid. As a first step try some of the things set out below.

MINI EXERCISES YOU CAN TRY IMMEDIATELY

- In your meetings, start to keep a tally of the ratio of questions to statements and the ratio of supportive comments to negative or blocking comments.

- Work over a period of weeks to adjust the balance, so that people are more supportive of each other and ask more incisive questions.

- Arrange for a total outsider to sit in on your next team problem-solving session. Take careful note of the different perspective that this brings and see how this impacts on the conversations you have.

- Count the number of open versus closed questions and leading versus non-leading questions that you and others ask.

- Look at your recruitment process – do you seek clones or do you seek diversity? What could you do to generate the selection of greater diversity in terms of background, approach and thinking style?

- Look at your current induction process and see what you can change so that you value the ideas that new people bring and give them a chance to share their experience.

- Organise a day a month in a different department or organisation for a period of at least six months.

- Book yourself on a study tour.

- Take out a subscription to a magazine or journal in a field of interest different from your own.

FURTHER FOOD FOR THE CURIOUS

- Vullings, R. and Heleven, M. (2015) *Not Invented Here: Cross-industry Innovation.* BIS Publishers, Amsterdam:

  - A book full of fascinating examples of ideas crossing boundaries to drive new innovation.

- Johnson, S. (2010) *Where Good Ideas Come From: The Natural History of Innovation.* Allen Lane, London, a division of Penguin:

- A fascinating read that charts the genesis of many great innovations and points to five key principles that underpin the development of all great ideas.

- Gratton, L. (2007) *Hot Spots: Why Some Companies Buzz with Energy and Innovation and Others Don't.* FT Prentice Hall, London:

  - This book points to four conditions that increase the likelihood that spontaneous innovation will flourish in organisations.

- Berger, W. (2014) *A More Beautiful Question: The Power of Inquiry to Spark Breakthrough Ideas.* Bloomsbury USA, New York:

  - A great read with many real-world examples of how asking different sorts of questions opens up amazing possibilities.

- Poetz, M., Franke, N. and Schreier, M. (2014) 'Sometimes the Best Ideas Come from Outside Your Industry'. *Harvard Business Review,* November. Available from https://hbr.org/2014/11/sometimes-the-best-ideas-come-from-outside-your-industry [3 November 2017]:

  - A short and interesting article that points to practical ways in which you can search analogous or distant analogous fields to find solutions to the intractable problems that you face today.

5 BEING SEEN AS SOMEONE WHO HELPS CHANGE TO HAPPEN

This chapter will explore how organisations and individuals react to changing circumstances. It will outline and introduce the various strategies that are consciously or unconsciously adopted in the face of change and points towards tangible things that you can do in your capacity as a team leader. Your aim must be to drive meaningful changes of practice and behaviour and hence contribute to enhancing your customer value proposition[8] and delivering increased customer benefit.

WHY IS THIS IMPORTANT?

Nothing is permanent except change. (Heraclitus, c. 500 BC)

We are in transition to a world where change is continuous; not just episodic. (Kotter, 2008)

Change is the one big certainty in our organisations. What makes us successful today is often the root of our failure tomorrow. The problem is that when organisations are faced with instability in the environment, it generates uncertainty, which in turn leads to higher levels of stress and anxiety. This, in turn, leads to the very human reaction of falling back on established and familiar patterns and solutions. Paradoxically, the very time we most need to be flexible and accepting of change tends to be the

---

[8] A business or marketing statement that sets out why a customer should purchase a particular good or service.

time when we are least emotionally equipped to deal with the possibility and consequences of change.

> In today's world, feeling contented with the status quo is a dangerous position to be in.

If organisations don't change they become extinct and if people don't change they become irrelevant or surplus to requirements as far as their organisations are concerned.

> Take Kodak for example: founded in 1888 it was best known for and held a dominant position in photographic film products. As a result of the decline in sales of photographic film it began to struggle in the late 1990s, and in 2012 eventually filed for bankruptcy. Even though the company was ahead of many others in the field of digital photography it still defined itself as a film company.

THE IMPACT OF THE ISSUE

It is a sad fact that most people and most organisations don't tend to seriously consider changing their behaviours until there is no other viable choice, and when you get to that point it is invariably too late.

Simply saying you need to be more proactive rather than reactive is not very helpful. What organisations need is people who can shine a light into the darkness and illuminate a new way forward – to be the pathfinder for others – to lead the way to new behaviours and practices. Such people tend to be called change agents; they are the people who are skilled at asking the difficult questions that challenge existing ways of thinking and working. But it is not enough just to ask difficult questions – you have to do so in a positive way that excites people about an alternative future and ignites in them a passion to be part of that future.

All organisations need change agents, but being a change agent is not a role; you don't get appointed by HR. Being an agent for change is just something that some people can do and if you are one of those people you are a precious asset and will be quickly recognised as such.

MAKING SENSE OF IT ALL

Change happens; your external environment can change in response to any number of independent or related variables over which you generally have little or no control. Your organisation will then find itself having to adapt to continue to function in that changing environment; the actions you take may be planned and deliberate, or you may just stumble into them almost by accident.

> The advent of technology has had a disruptive impact on many industries; consider what happened to the watch industry when digital watches first hit the market. Then we experienced new technology being replaced by even newer technology – consider the lifespan of the CD and DVD. The current wave of disrupters such as Uber and Airbnb do not own any assets; they are providing connectivity to a previously 'un-tappable' market. The future is poised to be even more profound with the possibilities that driverless cars, virtual, augmented and mixed reality, and a tactile internet among others may provide. The message is clear: change or die. Become the disrupter rather than the disrupted.

Change has always been with us; the only new thing is that our external environment may be changing more quickly than it used to, or may be prone to more violent and unanticipated swings. What has not changed much is the way that managers and leaders react to change. In broad terms, there are four types of leadership response:

- **Defender.** Leaders with this mindset tend to see little or no uncertainty in the environment. They are comfortable and feel a level of immunity to the turmoil that appears to beset others. Their response, if any, is to make minor adjustments in organisational structures or processes.

  - History tells us that this defensive stance leads to extinction.

- **Reactor.** Leaders with this mindset see that change and uncertainty exist, but will not initiate any response until they have overwhelming evidence that inaction is no longer an option. At this stage, they may make substantial adjustments, but generally they are too late to gain advantage and the result of their actions is merely a slowing of the rate of their corporate decline. This mentality leads to a protracted struggle for survival and the best outcome is an extended life in the margins.

- **Nimble mimic.** These leaders see change and uncertainty, but are reluctant to make the necessary investment of resources to deal with them. Instead, they perfect the art of waiting for someone else to find a solution, and then rapidly adopt and adapt that solution for their own ends.

  - This sort of stance ensures survival and can even produce growth, but such leaders are always playing catch-up and are always under threat from someone who can learn to copy better, faster or more cheaply.

- **Pioneer.** These leaders understand that change and uncertainty are constant companions. They continually experiment with new ways of responding to emerging trends. They are masters of intelligent opportunism. Pioneers have the ability to relate a proposed change to the business strategy or bigger picture and, in doing so, they can be instrumental in anchoring the change into new ways of working.

- Organisations and individuals who adopt this attitude will survive and prosper in any environment.

What we find interesting is that even companies which are, by nature, reactors or mimics still desire their managers to be pioneers. Indeed, a significant emphasis of many current leadership programmes is how to make managers more future-focused and innovative.

> Consider Apple. No one knew they wanted an 'iPod' until it had been invented. Steve Jobs anticipated the need. His view was that there was no point in asking a customer what they wanted – they didn't know until they saw it. His philosophy was to 'put a dent in the universe'. He believed that the people who are crazy enough to think they can change the world are the ones who do.

It appears then that the most valuable management skill is not the ability to react to and manage through change, but rather the ability to anticipate movements in the market and have capacity in place to take advantage as it is happening. The ability to anticipate in this way usually comes from a process of constantly watching and looking for opportunities, rather than as a result of genius.

> If you can show yourself to have a pioneering attitude towards change, you will be an invaluable asset to your organisation.

PRACTICAL ADVICE

There are no end of books that will help you understand the process of organisational change and the strategies that have proved to be successful for others. But most of them start from the assumption that you know what needs to be done and the main problem is how to make it happen successfully.

Our question has a little wider focus; we recognise that your organisation needs people who can:

- see opportunities for change that others can't see; this means being able to look upwards and outwards and, in effect, see the money that others are leaving on the table;

- see an opportunity and then devise a strategy to deliver the benefits and reap the subsequent rewards for the organisation;

- galvanise people and resources behind an initiative and make something happen;

- remain focused on the main chance and take advantage of serendipity along the way.

We have studied people who appear to be adept at leveraging these benefits for their organisations and identified a number of common characteristics that drive their actions. If you want to be seen as someone who makes change happen, we suggest that you take every opportunity to model the following behaviours.

Be someone who knows where they are going. Understand what is important for the long-term health of the business, how your business creates customer value and what you and your department can do to increase customer value in that context. What does the business model look like and where do you fit into it? What new capabilities or approaches can help transform or renew your business model? Pick one or two things that will become your focus for the next 18 months to 3 years. Make sure that your thinking is aligned with that of your boss and that you both want, and are driving towards, the same goals:

- Don't just blindly respond to short-term, flavour-of-the-month initiatives. Focus on things that will contribute to the wider, long-term goals of your organisation.

- Focus on the outcome. In all your discussions pull the thinking back to the outcome and create solid mental links between what is being done now and how it will build towards or enable the long-term goal.

- Don't get locked into a **quality** mentality of **right first time**, or thinking that there is one best solution to any problem; that approach works well for business as usual, but not for organisational change. When you are dealing with change you need a very flexible, iterative approach that values experimentation and recognises that failure is an essential component of success.

Bring the truth into the room. When you are dealing with issues that involve change, there are always at least three agendas at play: rational, personal and social. People are always comfortable about sharing their rational concerns and agenda, such as cost, resources and growth. They are less willing to share their personal and social concerns and agendas, yet you know that up to 80 per cent of their decision-making will be based on their personal and social agendas:

- Have the courage to say the unsayable, to ask the forbidden questions, confront the 'taboos' of the organisation and challenge the 'eternal truths' that are accepted about how things work around here.

- Don't shy away from uncomfortable conversations; they are both liberating and insightful.

- Get people to articulate their fears; getting them out in the open makes them less powerful.

- Get resistance out in the open; listen to people's concerns and issues and get them to engage in 'change talk'.

- Agree the facts of the situation. Often business issues that are raised turn out to be just personal issues that are dressed up. Get people to confront their own fears and give them a factual basis.

Utilise peer pressure. Work to create allies and advocates who will carry your message with passion and commitment:

- Provide your followers with an igniting purpose: a question, task or vision that engages their hearts as well as their minds and gives them a way of making a contribution that can stand the test of time. You also need to engage their heads by calling upon the unique skills, knowledge and experience that they possess and only they can bring to the venture.

- Recognise that change only happens when enough people think it is a good idea and they are prepared to invest their personal resources (and reputation) in the endeavour. You need to constantly expand your network of committed followers and connect them together, so that they can mutually support each other when you are not there.

Cultivate a predisposition towards action. All great successes are built on the back of constant experimentation and frequent failure:

- Start today. Do something now and see where it takes you. It is mind-numbingly time-consuming to sit around and discuss, debate and delay. Often there are no right answers, only choices, so make a choice and **do something**. If it takes you closer to where you want to go, then do more of the same; if not, then do something else. If you do something, you always have the opportunity to move forwards. If you don't do anything, you will always stand still or slip backwards.

- Adopt a relentless focus on a few (maximum two or three) key outcomes that you want to achieve and link every decision you make to its ability to get you a step closer to one of those key outcomes. Avoid long wish lists of activities; they can be overwhelming and a sense of being overwhelmed stops action.

- Be opportunistic! Often our actions have unintended or unanticipated consequences. Learn to sense those consequences and find ways of capitalising on those that could have a positive impact on what you are trying to achieve.

- If you think you need 'out-of-the-box' thinking, then get out of the box. Involve people from a different business unit, culture or industry; find people who see the world differently. Use their new eyes and ears to help you see new possibilities and to refine your own understanding of how you communicate about your vision and desired outcome.

Engage both hearts and minds. Communication can be directed at either the head (cognitive, supported by facts and figures) or the heart (affective, emotional, appealing to values). In his book, *The Heart of Change* (2002), John Kotter suggested that people don't change just because they think it is a good idea; they change because they have made an emotional commitment.

- Don't just communicate facts; let your passion show and don't be afraid of letting people see why something is so important to you.

- Don't talk at people; rather, engage in dialogue with them. Your aim is to gain committed behaviour, not compliant behaviour. When people are committed they give generously of their time and resources and they actively champion your cause, rather than watch from the sidelines.

- Connect people together and give them the space to use their talents to find new and novel ways of rising to the challenges you identify.

- Look for people who are full of ideas and dissatisfied with the way things are currently done. If you can harness their enthusiasm they can be a valuable resource. But make sure that you pair them up with someone who is 100 per cent aligned with what you are trying to achieve; otherwise you can find that the intellectually curious have wandered off down a different track. Passion combined with brains can produce great things, but generally you need someone else's hands on the steering wheel too.

Deal with the resistors. Not everyone can, or will, become an ally or advocate. Change always produces winners and losers and just hoping that people will come around is not a great option:

- Once you have a critical mass, some will follow the herd and get on side. You may need to neutralise others by bargaining with them or co-opting them onto the project. Find out what is important to them so that you can understand their price and the potential value they can bring.

- It is important that you don't let the resistors take up too much of your time. Pick them off one at a time and try to limit your overall effort in this area to no more than 25 per cent of your available time.

- If all else fails, make it clear that resistance is useless and propose a 'take it or leave it' deal. Manipulation, co-option or removal from the team may be your only options, but these tactics should only be used as a last resort.

- Ensure you operate 'fair process' and that you send a consistent message. The theory behind fair process is that people will buy into an outcome, even if it is less than ideal for them, as long as they agree with the process that led to that outcome and perceive it to be fair.

Celebrate your successes. Change is a tiring business and people need periods of rest and recuperation so that they can get ready to fight the next battle.

- Be generous with the way you recognise important contributions.

- Learn about what is working well, particularly around critical interpersonal relationships.

THINGS FOR YOU TO WORK ON NOW

We have pointed to a range of things that you can try in order to become more adept at seeing and exploiting opportunities to initiate and deliver change. We are not talking about change for the sake of change or change that is superficial in nature. What we need is change that drives your business forward and delivers benefits to your customers. In order to do this, your efforts need to be focused in the right direction. We suggest that you use the questions below to help you identify where you can start to make a real contribution.

KEY QUESTIONS TO ASK YOURSELF

?

- What two things do our customers value most about what we do, and how could we do those things better?

- If I had a completely free hand and no resource constraints, what are the two things I would change about the way we do our work?

- What two things give my team the most problems?

- Which problems never seem to get fixed and why?

- What are the big assumptions or 'eternal truths' about our company that nobody ever seems to challenge?

- What excites my team members and why?

- What drains the energy from my team members and why?

- What is the last thing our customers or competitors would think that we were capable of achieving and why?

Your answers to the above questions should help you focus on the key areas that can deliver benefit but you need to be clear that any change you devise must be consistent with the current business model. So, your first task is to really understand how your business creates value and what 'big assumptions' underpin the model. Try the exercises below to help you get a clearer picture of your customer value proposition. If you are unfamiliar with the idea of the business model we suggest that you first read through the Johnson, Christensen and Kagermann article listed in the resource section.

MINI EXERCISES YOU CAN TRY IMMEDIATELY

- Make sure that you understand the business model of your organisation and how your part of the business directly contributes to delivering the customer value proposition. Get to a level of understanding where you can sketch it on one side of A4 and explain how what you do contributes to the business as a whole.

- Reflect on the two or three big assumptions that underpin the business model. For each one, make a list of the behaviours that the assumption creates and think about how those behaviours could change if one or more of those assumptions changed.

- Look at your major competitors and see if you can work out what they are doing successfully that is different from you and how that could be incorporated into your own company's business model.

- Do a personal audit of your objectives for the next 12 months. How many of them are aimed at bringing about some fundamental change in your area of the organisation? For each one, identify the desired outcome and what impact it has on your customer value proposition, or how it contributes to accelerating the delivery of the business model.

FURTHER FOOD FOR THE CURIOUS

- Beavan, C. (2017) 'What It Takes to Change Hearts and Minds'. *Yes! Magazine.* Available from www.yesmagazine.org/issues/science/what-it-takes-to-change-hearts-and-minds-20170223 [18 July 2017]:

  - This short article contrasts communication that appeals to the mind with that which seeks to move people by inspiring and speaking to core values.

- Kotter, J.P. and Cohen, D.S. (2002) *The Heart of Change.* Harvard Business School Press, Boston, MA:

  - In the intervening years of research after the initial statement of the eight conditions of change in his previous book, *Leading Change* (1995), Kotter came to realise the importance of the human aspect and the need to appeal not only to the head but also to the heart. This book is more rounded and contains more examples of his ideas at work in organisations.

- Kotter, J.P. and Rathgeber, H. (2006) *Our Iceberg is Melting: Changing and Succeeding under Any Conditions.* MacMillan, London:

  - This is a retelling of the *Heart of Change* (2002) as a metaphor. It is simple to read and engaging, while losing none of the theoretical underpinning of his work.

- Johnson, M.W., Christensen, C.M. and Kagermann, H. (2008) 'Reinventing Your Business Model'. *Harvard Business Review*, December, 51–59:

  - This easy to read article sets out the key elements of a business model in terms of customer value proposition, key resources, key processes and profit formula. The article contains many illustrative examples that help clarify the concept.

6 HELPING YOUR TEAM TO COPE WITH THE RIGOURS OF CHANGE

The focus of this chapter is on the human side of change. It looks at why people resist change even when logically they can see that it is the right thing to do. Often technology fundamentally changes our relationship with our work and our working colleagues; it enables new ways of working, thinking and relating; and such all-embracing change can be disorientating. How people react to change is as much about what is already in their head as it is about the realities of the proposed change. In this chapter, we provide some critical insights about how you as a leader can help people through the various stages of change.

WHY IS THIS IMPORTANT?

For many people, the prospect of organisational change can trigger a strong, even overwhelming, sense of anxiety. In extreme cases, a department or even a whole organisation can drift into a state of listless near-paralysis. These are the conditions that often result in entrenched resistance to the idea of change and can be the death knell for new ways of working or the adoption of new behaviours. As a manager, your job is to guide your people through these turbulent times.

Most organisational change initiatives fail to produce the outcomes that were hoped for at the outset. Sometimes this is because the environment moves on again and the change is no longer relevant, but more often the issue is that not enough people really appreciated the need to change or actively refuse to change before significant damage has occurred. Once you get to that stage, change is like pushing a rock uphill; it is difficult, exhausting and essentially futile, and if you let up for a moment, it will roll back and squash you.

Many IT functions recognise the need for and benefit of collaboration. For example, a project is launched to assess and introduce various collaborative tools. From an IT perspective the project is seen as successful; however, the business fails to derive much benefit. The tools are underutilised and when they are used they are often populated with the wrong type of information. People need to share and to collaborate; there needs to be an environment of trust; egos and power through knowledge need to be put aside. Tools are useful only where a collaborative mindset is already in place.

To be successful at preparing people for change you have to start the process before they even get the idea that a change may be needed. In the same way that a gardener spends time enriching and preparing the soil in flower beds long before the time comes to plant out the seedlings, you, as a manager, need to work to create a state of readiness for change. You need to give your team the tools and the attitudes to see the positives in prospective changes and the will to take action and make those changes a working reality.

THE IMPACT OF THE ISSUE

Change is now an ever-present feature of organisational life, yet our understanding of how to bring about change in human systems is still tenuous, and many managers feel ill-equipped to deal with the human fallout from their change initiatives.

The thinking behind how to bring about and manage organisational change has moved on considerably in the last 20 years and now most managers appreciate that change is a process; however, most of the models used to guide managers view change as something that you do to other people, or other systems. Yes, such models emphasise the importance of taking people with you, having a vision, communicating urgency, building a network of committed people and so on. Yet, laudable though all this is, they are still stuck in the belief that change is something done to others. The reality is that where human behaviour is concerned change can only come from the inside; each and every individual must come to the decision to change for themselves, and for each person the trigger for that change will be different.

A development manager was struggling with getting his staff to accept that they would have to physically move desks as a result of a departmental reorganisation. Everyone agreed on the need for people to move as long as it wasn't happening to them. Some people feared losing their window seat, while others were concerned about who they would be sitting next to. In order to unblock the situation, the manager gave his staff the new floor plan for their allocated area along with pens, Post-its and pizza and gave them a totally free hand in sorting out who would sit where. Within three hours they had it all sorted out with everyone in agreement with the new arrangements.

When faced with change, very few people will find it exciting and exhilarating, and a similarly small proportion will become very active and vocal opponents of anything that looks different. But the **normal** reaction to change is **ambivalence**. Let's be clear about this, ambivalence does not mean 'doesn't care'. To be ambivalent is to simultaneously hold two opposing and conflicting attitudes or emotions. Because change is all around us, most people have learned to be ambivalent until they understand how the proposed change will affect them at a personal level. You have a position where people cannot motivate themselves to change unless and until their very personal ambivalence is resolved.

So, at any given time, most of the people who work for you will be ambivalent to change. This means that they are subconsciously caught in a conflict of opposing attitudes and emotions that results in competing commitments. These competing commitments will undermine morale and performance and could, ultimately, paralyse any change initiative. The following story illustrates such a conflict:

> George, a BRM (business relationship manager), truly believed in and was committed to a collaborative approach. However, the company policy of 'stack ranking' meant that collaboration might give the advantage to someone else in an environment where employees were competing for their jobs and possibly their livelihood. Stack ranking is the process whereby managers across a company are required to rank employee performance on a bell curve; typically 10 per cent are designated as high performers, those labelled as low performers are often fired or pushed out. This practice is far more common in the US than in the UK.

In George's case, he achieved a number of small wins but failed to achieve any significant change either to the culture of the organisation or in the behaviour of its people. George therefore left the organisation for another where the culture allowed him to make a significant contribution that benefited his new organisation as a whole.

MAKING SENSE OF IT ALL

People react to change, or the threat of change, at an emotional level. Change evokes strong emotions and that internal turmoil tends to produce observable behaviour patterns. Much of the thought about human change comes from working with people undergoing profound change; often this work has been done by clinical psychologists working with people coping with bereavement, terminal illness or substance abuse and dependency. These ideas are then picked up, generalised and reshaped to fit the world of organisational behaviour.

The most widely known model comes from pioneering work carried out by Elizabeth Kübler-Ross and published in her book *On Death and Dying* (1969). In this she identifies five stages of transition for people facing death, namely denial, anger, bargaining, depression and, finally, acceptance. She was at pains to stress that the order of these stages is not necessarily chronological; nor will everyone experience all five stages. It is also not a linear process – people don't progress neatly from one stage to the next; they experience setbacks and can flip from stage to stage.

The model was quickly appropriated by organisational psychologists and subsequently expanded, and is often now termed the **change cycle** or the **change roller coaster**. A typical representation of the roller coaster is shown in Figure 6.1.

There can be no doubt that the Kübler-Ross curve is a valuable insight into the human response to change, but, sadly, the change roller coaster concept has been widely shared by people with no understanding of where it comes from or its underpinning philosophy. The result is that too many managers wrongly believe that this is some form of mechanistic process where everyone goes through all the stages in this order, and that their role as a manager is to help their people get through the stages as quickly as possible. Such a belief is less than helpful and can do irreparable harm to people who are in a vulnerable emotional state.

The reality is that each person will experience change differently depending upon their individual hopes, fears and personal disposition.

Most of us can cope with a few changes at one time, but for each of us there comes a time when we reach a tipping point where we fail to cope. At this point, we can become overwhelmed with ambivalence as a sort of defence mechanism.

More recent work has focused on trying to understand the root causes of personal ambivalence or, in the words of Kegan and

Figure 6.1 Behaviour through the transition curve⁹

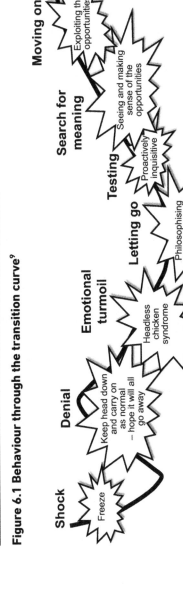

⁹ Behaviour through the transition curve is based on an adaptation of the grief cycle, devised and published by Elizabeth Kübler-Ross (1969) in her seminal work, *On Death and Dying*, first published in the UK by Tavistock Publications Ltd in 1970.

Lahey (2001; see the 'Further food for the curious' section at the end of this chapter), 'competing commitments'. This is the idea that people's backgrounds, early experiences, education and so on cause them to adopt 'big assumptions' about how the world works. These mental frameworks are often unexamined and unconscious, but they colour everything we see and generate the internal competing commitments. A competing commitment may blindside us to the need for change, or paralyse us into a state of confused inaction where we know that we need to change, but cannot find the motivation to do so, or to maintain our course of action.

Current thinking indicates that in order for people to find the motivation to change they need help to surface and confront their competing commitments.

It is becoming clear that people don't change because they hear your words, no matter how eloquent and persuasive they may be; they change when they take part in a discussion about their own competing commitments and the roots of their ambivalence. This sort of discussion is called **change talk** and is at the heart of a technique practised by clinical psychologists called **motivational interviewing**. Getting people to engage in change talk is a critical element of motivational interviewing. We recognise that it is unrealistic, and possibly dangerous, to expect managers to become amateur clinical psychologists. However, it is reasonable to expect managers to understand that their role is not to **talk at their people** about change, but rather to **openly engage their people in change talk** in such a way as to allow them to surface and explore their own competing concerns and commitments. Through this understanding, they can find a route to their own motivation to change.

PRACTICAL ADVICE

If you have had any change management training, you have probably come to view organisational change as a process.

Typically, that process will have four or five stages; for example, the eight factors for successful change that are set out in Kotter's book *Our Iceberg is Melting* (2006) can be mapped into a model of four phases: setting the scene, deciding what to do, making it happen and making it stick.

Helpful and insightful though this is, you must remember that this is a model of how you implement change, not how people respond to change.

If we are looking for a model that maps this change process, but explicitly deals with human reaction to change, it would be better to take the five-stage model that underpins motivational interviewing and the world of competing commitments. The Stages of Change model[10] helps those making an organisational change to keep on track and to embrace best practice in change management. It identifies the five stages of change as being:

     i.   pre-thinking;
    ii.   thinking;
   iii.   deciding;
   iv.   doing;
    v.   maintaining.

The model reminds you of your role as the leader of your people during change.

The manager's role and approach differs in each of the stages. Yes, you need to do all the things associated with the process model of change, but, in addition, you should be working on a one-to-one basis with your people to help you understand their motivations and engage in change talk. Here is some general guidance on how to approach each of the stages.

---

[10] The Stages of Change Model was originally developed in the late 1970s and early 1980s by James Prochaska and Carlo DiClemente (1983) at the University of Rhode Island in their work on addiction. This model now underpins many approaches used in helping people to bring about fundamental behavioural changes.

Pre-thinking stage. When people are in this stage they are not yet considering change, or are unwilling, or unable, to accept that change may be necessary. The manager's role is to:

- Start to raise doubt in their minds that things can go on as they are.

- Give them information about the risks and problems they face; give concrete examples of how the same sorts of problems have beset other departments, companies or industries and the consequential fallout from these issues. Involve them in brainstorming and prioritising the risks that could impact your change initiative.

- Bring an awareness of the outside to the inside. This form of open and honest communication about the changing world and our place in it will reduce the shock that we tend to experience at the start of the change curve.

Thinking stage. Now people can see the possibility of change, but are ambivalent about the change. They cannot find within them the motivation to begin the change journey and remain uncertain and unconvinced that it is the right thing for them. This is the time when you need to engage in real change talk:

- Bring the reasons for ambivalence to the surface.

- Discover together the big assumptions that are held about how things work and what their place is in the scheme of things.

- Avoid being judgemental.

- Don't take sides, but do encourage people to challenge their own beliefs and support them in the process through reflective questioning, affirmation and summarising. This will help people to get through the denial phase of the change curve.

Deciding stage. They are now convinced of the need to change and are motivated to do so, but remain unclear about what they need to do and how they should go about it. This is a critical stage and the manager now has a role to:

- Help them think through what they might do first. Maybe create a simple plan of things they can do tomorrow or next week; avoid the long term and keep things low key.
- Explore with them through questioning and active listening what they might do if things don't go to plan.
- Use reflective listening and affirmation to help them through the emotional turmoil of the change curve.

Doing stage. They are now actively taking steps to achieve the change, but their steps are hesitant and faltering; they have not yet stabilised themselves into new routines and patterns of thinking and are prone to doubt and uncertainty. As a manager, you can help:

- Help them to be realistic about what they can achieve and to plan in terms of small steps.
- Use open questions and affirmation to help them develop coping strategies when they experience frustration and setbacks.
- Help them look for opportunities to reinforce positive behaviours and anchor them in their daily routines. Discuss openly things that are good about the new ways of working and things that are not so good; avoid being judgemental.
- Give them support and guidance and the resources they need to experiment with new ideas and ways of working. They are now letting go of their old ways and a key element will be the space to try out new things and help when they hit speed bumps and roadblocks.

Maintaining stage. They have now achieved the change goals they set themselves and are working to sustain the new patterns of behaviour and ways of thinking and seeing the world. As a manager, your role now is to help:

- Maintain supportive contact.

- Monitor progress against personal objectives and help to set new short- and medium-term goals.

- Help them to find new meaning and motivation as they settle into new working patterns and practices.

- Help them to increase their circle of influence, so that they can create a new support network for themselves.

As you try to help your staff through the phases of change, you will find that you increasingly need to call upon and develop four key skills. Fortunately, these are not new skills; they are the same skills that you use to coach, provide feedback, delegate and facilitate group problem solving. They are:

- **Open-ended questioning.** This is how you get change talk going. Use question structures such as:

  - How would you like things to be different?

  - What would you be able to achieve if we could take 'x' out of the way?

  - What are the good things about the current situation and what are the not so good things about it?

- **Affirming statements.** This is an important skill and is not just about saying nice things or flattering people. Your aim is to:

  - Recognise strength when you see it. Sometimes it is easier for you to see that they have made a big step than it is for them to see that they have moved.

  - Share with them the things that they have done that you really appreciate and would like them to do more of. Get them to give similar feedback to you.

  - Once you have built a trusting relationship move on to talk about the things that they are doing that are less effective and that you would like them to do less of. Similarly, you can have a discussion about the effectiveness of your own behaviours.

  - Build their confidence in their own ability to change.

- Be genuine and make sure that your actions, words and body language all match.

- **Reflective listening.** When you ask questions you need to become very good at listening. You also need to show that you are listening and understanding them by reflecting back what you hear:

  - In the first instance, stick to simple reflection – repeat and rephrase what they have told you, sticking as closely to their words as possible.

  - Later, and if you suspect that there may be a deeper meaning behind the words being used, you can start to work towards amplified reflection. This is where you paraphrase and then use gentle probing or analytical questions to find out what's going on below the surface. In such cases, how you say things is as important as what you say. Avoid any form of words that might convey judgement or cast doubt on their right to hold and express the views that they have.

- **Summarising.** This is a special case of reflective listening and generally is used as a transition point in a conversation. You might use structures such as:

  - Let me see if I understand what you are saying ...

  - I think what you are saying is ... in which case that might lead us to consider how we might ...

Practise these four key skills, but remember the context in which you use them will determine how you use them.

THINGS FOR YOU TO WORK ON NOW

Below are some questions that will help you build a picture of how tuned in you are to the emotional and psychological effects of change, whether it affects your team members, your customers or clients or your business partners. It is not enough to be technically capable and good at managing processes;

business benefit is always delivered through people, and as a leader you need to be able to support people as they wrestle with the competing commitments that inhibit fundamental and lasting change.

Reflect on your answers to the above questions and pick one aspect to work on over the next few weeks. To make this real you need to think about your approach within the context of a real organisational change that you have worked through recently.

KEY QUESTIONS TO ASK YOURSELF

- How much time do I actually spend listening to the concerns of my team members? Not just fobbing them off, but really listening.

- How good am I at picking up on the concerns and feelings of the people in my team and immediate working environment?

- If this is not a natural ability for me, who can I turn to that I trust who has a natural sense of empathy, and how can I work with them to compensate for my own lack of awareness?

- What are my own 'big assumptions' and consequential competing commitments?

- How much of my time do I spend getting people ready for the possibility of change?

Below are some suggestions about things you can work on that will help you to better understand your own subconscious drivers and the possible effects of your behaviour on others. This sort of deep critical reflection is not easy and you may find it best to work on these ideas with someone with whom you have a strong, trust-based relationship.

MINI EXERCISES YOU CAN TRY IMMEDIATELY

- Do a personal audit on a recent change that has impacted your team. What was your role in that change? How did people react to the change and to your role? Was the pattern of the change 'decide – announce – defend', or was it more in the form of 'consult – decide – sell'?

- Read the recommended article 'The Real Reason People Won't Change' (Kegan and Lahey, 2001); study the table that takes you through the questions to uncover your competing commitments and their underpinning big assumptions. Do the exercise for yourself.

- Now you have a clearer idea of your own competing commitments, reflect on how your own big assumptions can get in the way of you seeing opportunities to change and be different.

- Practise reflective listening when talking to one of your team members about a new skill or task you want them to step up to. Afterwards, ask them for feedback on how they felt when you summarised their thoughts and made affirmative statements.

If you are inspired to find out more about any of the themes covered in this chapter we suggest that you start by reviewing the resources listed below.

FURTHER FOOD FOR THE CURIOUS

- Robinson, T. (2017) 'Helping People Change'. *Training Journal*, July, 16–17:
  - This short article contains 10 tips for helping people change.

- Kegan, R. and Lahey, L. (2001) 'The Real Reason People Won't Change'. *Harvard Business Review*, November, 84–92:

  - This article introduces the idea of competing commitments: subconscious hidden goals that compete with their stated commitments. It is an interesting paper that will make you examine why you believe the things you do, how you came to believe them and how those beliefs can constrain your options for action.

- Miller, W.R. and Rollnick, S. (2012) *Motivational Interviewing: Helping People Change* (3rd edn). Guilford Publications, New York:

  - This is not for the faint-hearted, but for anyone who is serious about finding out more on the subject of motivational interviewing this is a great place to start.

- Kotter, J.P. and Rathgeber, H. (2006) *Our Iceberg is Melting: Changing and Succeeding under Any Conditions*. Macmillan, London:

  - This is a retelling of Kotter's earlier work, *The Heart of Change* (2002), using an ecological metaphor. It is simple to read and engaging, while losing none of the theoretical underpinning of his previous work. It is an ideal text to give to your team members to help them focus on the stages of change and the challenges.

BIBLIOGRAPHY

Beavan, C. (2017) 'What It Takes to Change Hearts and Minds'. *Yes! Magazine.* Available from www.yesmagazine. org/issues/science/what-it-takes-to-change-hearts-and-minds-20170223 [18 July 2017].

Berger, W. (2014) *A More Beautiful Question: The Power of Inquiry to Spark Breakthrough Ideas.* Bloomsbury USA, New York.

Bhaskar, M. (2016) *Curation: The Power of Selection in a World of Excess.* Piatkus Press, London.

Bowman, N. (2016) '4 Ways to Improve Your Strategic Thinking Skills'. *Harvard Business Review*, December. Available from https://hbr.org/2016/12/4-ways-to-improve-your-strategic-thinking-skills [3 November 2017].

Chatham, R. (2015) *The Art of IT Management: Practical Tools, Techniques and People Skills.* BCS, Swindon.

Chatham, R. and Sutton, B. (2010) *Changing the IT Leader's Mindset: Time for Revolution rather than Evolution.* IT Governance Publishing, Cambridge.

Chatham, R., Mead, K. and Moschella, D. (2016) *Raising IT's Game through BRM.* Leading Edge Forum, London.

Christensen, C.M., Cook, S. and Hall, T. (2005) 'Marketing Malpractice: The Cause and the Cure'. *Harvard Business Review*, December: 74–83.

Collins, J. (2005) 'Level 5 Leadership: The Triumph of Humility and Fierce Resolve'. *Harvard Business Review*, July–August. Available from https://hbr.org/2005/07/level-5-leadership-the-triumph-of-humility-and-fierce-resolve [3 November 2017].

Covey, S.R. (2004) *The 7 Habits of Highly Effective People: Powerful Lessons in Personal Change.* Simon & Schuster, London.

Davey, L. (2014) 'Strengthen your Strategic Thinking Muscles'. *Harvard Business Review*, January. Available from https://hbr.org/2014/01/strengthen-your-strategic-thinking-muscles [3 November 2017].

Day, G.S. and Schoemaker, P.J.H. (2006) *Peripheral Vision: Detecting the Weak Signals that Will Make or Break Your Company.* Harvard Business School Press, Boston, MA.

Dixon, M., Freeman, K. and Toman, N. (2010) 'Stop Trying to Delight Your Customers'. *Harvard Business Review*, July–August. Available from https://hbr.org/2010/07/stop-trying-to-delight-your-customers [3 November 2017].

Dixon, M., Ponomareff, L., Turner, S. and DeLisi, R. (2017) 'Kick-Ass Customer Service'. *Harvard Business Review*, January–February. Available from https://hbr.org/2017/01/kick-ass-customer-service [3 November 2017].

Gratton, L. (2007) *Hot Spots: Why Some Companies Buzz with Energy and Innovation and Others Don't.* FT Prentice Hall, London.

Hammer, M. (2001) *The Agenda: What Every Business Must Do to Dominate the Decade.* Random House, New York.

Hayashi, A.M. (2001) 'When to Trust Your Gut'. *Harvard Business Review*, February. Available from https://hbr.org/2001/02/when-to-trust-your-gut [3 November 2017].

Ingvar, D.H. (1985) 'Memory of the Future: An Essay on the Temporal Organisation of the Conscious Awareness'. *Human Neurobiology*, 4(3), 127–136.

Johnson, M.W., Christensen, C.M. and Kagermann, H. (2008) 'Reinventing Your Business Model'. *Harvard Business Review*, December, 51–59.

Johnson, S. (2010) *Where Good Ideas Come From: The Natural History of Innovation*. Allen Lane, London, a division of Penguin.

Kegan, R. and Lahey, L.L. (2001) 'The Real Reason People Won't Change'. *Harvard Business Review*, November, 84–92.

Kotter, J.P. and Cohen, D.S. (2002) *The Heart of Change: Real-life Stories of How People Change Their Organizations*. Harvard Business School Press, Boston, MA.

Kotter, J.P. and Rathgeber, H. (2006) *Our Iceberg is Melting: Changing and Succeeding under Any Conditions* (1st edn). Macmillan, London.

Kübler-Ross, E. (1969) *On Death and Dying*. Routledge, London.

Losada, M. and Heaphy, E. (2004) 'The Role of Positivity and Connectivity in the Performance of Business Teams: A Nonlinear Dynamics Model'. *American Behavioral Scientist*, 47(6), 740–765. doi: 10.1177/0002764203260208

Miller, W.R. and Rollnick, S. (2012) *Motivational Interviewing: Helping People Change* (3rd edn). Guilford Publications, New York.

Patching, K. and Chatham, R. (2000) *Corporate Politics for IT Managers: How to Get Streetwise*. Routledge, London.

Poetz, M., Franke, N. and Schreier, M. (2014) 'Sometimes the Best Ideas Come from Outside Your Industry'. *Harvard Business Review*, November. Available from https://hbr.org/2014/11/sometimes-the-best-ideas-come-from-outside-your-industry [3 November 2017].

Prochaska, J.O. and DiClemente, C.C. (1983) 'Stages and Processes of Self-change of Smoking: Toward an Integrative Model of Change'. *Journal of Consulting and Clinical Psychology*, 51(3), 390–395. doi: 10.1037/0022-006X.51.3.390

Reichheld, F.F. (2003) *The One Number You Need to Grow*. Harvard Business School Press, Boston, MA.

Robinson, T. (2017) 'Helping People Change'. *Training Journal*, July, 16–17.

Tapscott, D. and Caston, A. (1993) *Paradigm Shift: The New Promise of Information Technology*. McGraw-Hill, New York.

Vullings, R. and Heleven, M. (2015) *Not Invented Here: Cross-industry Innovation*. BIS Publishers, Amsterdam.

INDEX